The Astrologer's Guide to Counseling

The
Astrologer's Guide to Counseling

Astrology's Role in the Helping Professions

Bernard Rosenblum, M.D.

CRCS Publications
Post Office Box 20850
Reno, Nevada 89515
U.S.A.

Library of Congress Cataloging in Publication Data

Rosenblum, Bernard, 1925–
    The astrologer's guide to counseling.

    1. Astrology and psychotherapy.   I. Title.
BF1729.P83R67 1982   133.5'81583   82-45631
ISBN 0-916360-14-8

FIRST EDITION
INTERNATIONAL STANDARD BOOK NUMBER: 0-916360-14-8
LIBRARY OF CONGRESS CATALOG CARD NUMBER: 82-045631
Published simultaneously in the United States and Canada by:
CRCS Publications
Distributed in the United States and internationally by
CRCS Publications
(Write for current list of worldwide distributors.)
Cover Design: Image & lettering both by Rebecca Wilson

Acknowledgements

I would like to thank, first of all, Barbara Somerfield and Henry Weingarten for their suggestion that I write this book and for their support. Discussions with Alan Epstein have been essential to the overall conceptualization of the first part of the book. Lynne Ericksson and Richard Idemon have been most helpful with suggestions and encouragement.

The astrology/psychology sharing group to which I belong has provided a rich source of ideas and mutuality. I therefore wish to thank each of its members: Allen Epstein, Charles Emerson, Joanna Shannon, Julian Armistead, Joan Negus, Ken Negus, Pat Morimando, Betty Lunstead, Nona Press, Lenore Canter, Faith McInerny, John Marchesella, and Allison Diamond.

I would particularly like to express my appreciation for the outstanding job of editing that Dodie Gerson Edmands has done. An astrologer and published author herself, she is on her way to becoming a psychotherapist and will, I expect, become one of the fine new healers of our coming age who combine astrology and psychotherapy.

Contents

Preface   1

Introduction   3

Part I: Astrology: Its Uses and Abuses

CHAPTER   1. The Contribution of Astrology
to Psychological Growth   7

          2. Psychological Dilemmas in
the Practice of Astrology   17

          3. The Astrologer's Confusing Role   24

          4. The Three Forms of Astrology   33

          5. The Growth of Astrology
as a Psychological Tool   45

Part II: Counseling and Psychotherapy: An Introduction for Astrologers

          6. Methods of Counseling   53

          7. General Psychotherapeutic Procedures   67

Part III: Common Astrological Counseling Problems: A Psychotherapist's View

          8. The Troubled Love Relationship   89

          9. The Dependent Client   95

        10. The Depressed Client   103

        11. The Client with Serious
Psychopathology   113

        12. Problems Created by the Astrologer   120

Conclusion: Astrology and Psychotherapy Revisited   131

The Astrologer's Guide to Counseling

Astrology's Role in the
Helping Professions

Preface

This book is written from the point of view of a psychotherapist who believes that good astrology can make a profound contribution to the growth of the spirit and consciousness of people today. It can be of significant assistance to the psychotherapist in particular, and in various ways, the most important being the excellent psychological overview of the patient that it provides.

At the same time, astrologers' work with clients, as excellent as it sometimes is, could definitely stand to be improved by a greater understanding of counseling skills. Acquisition of some of the important insights from the major psychological thinkers and schools of therapy can only add to the fuller vision and effectiveness of the astrologer. My aim is to make a start in this direction.

This book is not an effort to teach astrologers how to counsel more effectively in individual cases. Only an experienced astrologer with additional training in counseling and psychology can do that. It is, rather, an effort to explore some of the basic issues and dynamics involved, to raise questions—not give answers. If I have managed to clarify the role and function of the astrologer within the larger domain of the helping/healing arts and to bring the astrologer some insights from psychotherapy, my task will have been accomplished.

I hope the reader understands that many of the chapters contained herein are brief statements about large issues and that each really deserves an entire book in itself.

Introduction

The first time I went to an astrologer I was forty-one years old and had managed to ignore the subject up to then. Although I was interested in the humanities, what little I knew about astrology seemed to reveal it to be a pseudo-science filled with interesting generalities and unfounded predictions. Besides, I was becoming a scientist, a psychiatrist, and had to look at hard facts and realities. What did emotional disturbances, which supposedly have their origin in the first years of life, primarily in the child-parent relationship, have to do with the position of the sun, moon, and planets in relation to the earth at the time of a person's birth? Obviously, astrology had to be an unfounded and mystical theory.

But in the year or two preceding I had begun to question many of my philosophical assumptions about life. Perhaps there was more to life than the chance meeting between sperm and egg, the events that seem to occur haphazardly over the course of a life, and the solitary lifetime during which one feels so great a potential and so little time to accomplish it all. My consultation with an astrologer was part of the opening of my awareness to wider possibilities of viewing life than the rational, deterministic science of the day allowed.

I introduced myself to the astrologer as "mister," not "doctor," and took note that she was not observing me for clues. After fifteen minutes or so, during which time she described my personality patterns, she went on to say that I was, or should be, a psychoanalyst or psychiatrist. She even described something more specific about the type of therapy or analysis I would likely practice, which corresponded exactly to the orientation I had as a psychiatrist! At this point, I certainly had my money's worth and could have gone home satisfied, at least in the sense that I was very impressed with the accuracy of what an astrologer can find out about a person and with the philosophical implications of that ability. What I was later to discover was that this excellent "divining" and counseling tool can not only solve problems, but it can also present problems, both to astrologers and to their clients.

This initial, firsthand experience with astrology brought me face to face with valid statements about major areas of conflict in my life, areas of talent and other capabilities, my personal type of thinking and style of communication, how I spontaneously tend to relate to the world and to my unconscious and emotional life, my parental images, the way in which I relate to the opposite sex, and much more. It was all pointedly meaningful to me—and surprisingly specific. The usual criticism of astrology, that it produces a variety of generalities that can refer to almost anyone, was suddenly, in my mind, relevant only to newspaper and magazine types of astrology and no longer to the experience of going to a competent astrologer who uses all the astrological data at his or her disposal.

Now that I have studied the subject myself, I am well aware of the excellent contributions astrology can make to human understanding. Unfortunately, truly good-quality astrological counseling and writing are not easy to come by. The reasons behind the various difficulties experienced in the field of astrological counseling are the subject of this book.

Part I

Astrology: Its Uses and Abuses

1

The Contribution of Astrology to Psychological Growth

Although it has been used and abused for years as a fortune-telling device, astrology is at last beginning to be recognized as a tool for understanding the depth psychology of the individual in terms of cosmic principles. Derived from ancient sources, astrology has grown and changed over the centuries, always reflecting the culture of the time.

Modern psychotherapy, though it had its roots in the philosophy, literature, and natural sciences of the nineteenth and early twentieth centuries, was essentially born out of the great achievements of Sigmund Freud, C. G. Jung, and Wilhelm Reich. Their combined work has resulted in the foundation of an understanding of the modern psyche in the Western world and in a growing number of techniques for the healing of psychological imbalances. Psychotherapy, like astrology, is predicated on depth psychology, which presupposes that the psyche is complex, multidimensional, and partly unconscious. But unlike astrology, psychotherapy aims at the cure of the dysfunctions and imbalances of the psychological life through a procedure of regular consultations.*

---

*In my practice, I proceed from the point of view that the psychology of the individual is more than just mental attitudes. It includes the emotions, the sexual nature, the body, and a spiritual component. This is, of course, an artificial breakdown of what is actually a unitary energy manifesting in diverse phases. It is the same energy that Yoga philosophy calls *prana* and *kundalini* and that Reich calls *orgone energy*.

Both astrology and modern psychotherapy describe deep and essential aspects of the personality, but from different vantage points on the prism of the self. As diverse as the various psychotherapies are, they all offer both a theory of psychological imbalance and specific techniques to restore that balance. The focus is on the *healing* of the disturbed state, whether it be neurosis or psychosis. (The Jungian and Reichian approaches believe in an essential healthy core beneath the disturbed state.) Astrology, on the other hand, though it fully describes the painful and unbalanced emotional conditions of people and the need for greater internal harmony, puts more emphasis on the *inner meaning* of all aspects of experience, including suffering.

Depth psychotherapy* essentially treats emotional ills as the by-products of an unhealthy culture and mistaken child-rearing practices, insufficiencies that need to be corrected in order to regain the healthy potential of the individual. From the perspective of astrology, however, there are no mistakes. Astrology seems to say that the disturbing influences that arise during the course of growing up have an important meaning for soul growth and are not just errant misfortune. It teaches that the individual literally needs certain lessons of self-realization and soul correction and that he or she receives these through the particular balance of pleasurable and hurtful early experiences. The astrologer attempts to help the individual resolve and transform conflict and imbalance but at the same time works to understand the use and meaning of these impediments to freedom and gratification.

Both astrology and psychotherapy are valid for today's world. Yet only rarely have they met to exchange understanding and service. Astrologers have more respect for psychotherapy generally, especially the Jungian approach, than do psychotherapists for astrology. Astrology can be of real help

---

*By *depth psychotherapy* I am referring to those approaches that accept and work with the notion of an unconscious and that see the average person as presenting a surface personality to the world while a deeper part is hidden.

to psychotherapy because of its ability to reveal a comprehensive picture of a person's psychological structure and because of the deep understanding it affords of the cyclic patterns of the life stages. Psychotherapy can help the astrologer by providing other dimensions of psychological understanding not possessed by astrology, as well as by supplying techniques of counseling that can aid astrologers in their work.

In an attempt, therefore, to integrate the two fields, let me begin by examining some of the ways in which astrology can heal.

Self-Recognition

The first basic function of good astrology is to aid people in the development of self-recognition on a deep level. When the client is open enough to face some basic truths, and when the astrological material is presented with consideration for his or her capacities and sensitivities, that person feels uniquely perceived and affirmed. In fact, the very laying of one's psychological cards on the table, face up, the weaknesses and difficulties revealed along with the strong trump cards, usually brings relief and hope.

The horoscope generally reveals to us what we already know, but dimly, or just in pieces, and thus brings to a sharp focus the integrated whole of our being so that we can truly recognize ourselves. Relative order and simplicity are achieved out of the complexity of experiences, attitudes, and feelings of an individual, without oversimplifying human dynamics. Of course, familiarization with the astrological overview does not mean that the client now possesses the utmost in deep psychological understanding of the self. This will take increasing awareness of life experience as well as conscious work on the self, sometimes with the aid of therapy. What the overview can do is to provide a meaningful sense of direction as the process of self-understanding begins to unfold and take shape.

Self-Validation

Why is it easier for some people to understand themselves in the presence of an astrologer than in an interchange with a therapist, friend, family, or even through introspection? The reason is that in these latter situations we feel the need to live up to an ideal that is not always attainable. This sets up the potential for criticism from others or from oneself, and with that the sense that one needs to defend oneself. A vicious cycle ensues. This conflict, which is usually unconscious, represents the split between the ideal and the actual.

In the process of learning from an astrologer accurate generalities that describe ourselves, we acquire the feeling that we have an identity that is simultaneously objective, in that it is displayed on a piece of paper, yet that corresponds to our felt life experience. From this, we can begin really to look at ourselves with a greater sense of ease, even though we may still have serious inner difficulties. The internal split between the ideal and the real can then begin to heal simultaneously. Thus, because this method of self-recognition has a certain objectivity, a sense of self-validation and self-acceptance can begin to grow. Psychotherapists have generally found that clients cannot overcome difficult traits unless they fully accept the fact that they have them, thereby reducing the guilt and self-criticism that actually prevent correction of the undesirable qualities. An astrologer, Nona Press, described the process succinctly:

> Astrological clients come to feel self-accepting because they are described in a way they have always sensed was their true nature but felt was perverse, sick, or capricious. It may sound odd, but when we come to feel it is our nature to be a certain way, the door is open to working on and changing that "nature." Once we recognize and accept our basic qualities, we feel freer to change them. What before we may have thought of as "weird" about ourselves now feels natural. The natural thing one can work with, but not the weird.

Meaning and Direction

As people come to feel more self-affirming and accepting of their own internal life, they develop a greater sense of meaning about what they are undergoing in their periodic crises and day-to-day experiences. The horoscope might reveal, for example, an inner conflict in the perception and expression of a vital need, such as love, ego assertion, or communicative skills. With this revelation, the person no longer needs to feel that his block or his suffering are the result only of his being the helpless victim of such outside forces as a repressive society or neurotic parents. Instead, the client learns that the conflict has a purpose in the development of his psyche.

For example, a woman might have an inclination, inborn from karmic soul development, to be too accommodating in love relationships. Perhaps this tendency is reinforced by identification with a similar quality in her mother during childhood development. This situation could be reflected in the horoscope of a person with Venus in Libra* and other associated natal qualities. If no conflict were present in the chart in relation to this woman's Venus energies, she might remain an excessively accommodating person, neglecting her own needs. With a Saturn square to Venus, however, this tendency would bring into her life a good deal of frustration, so that the self-denial would not pay off emotionally. The woman would thus be challenged to modify the imbalance in favor of a healthier adaptation, even though there would be frustration and pain in the process. In other words, implicit in astrology is the view that there are checks and balances and that there is, in the long run, an inherent meaningfulness to our natal tendencies, including the pain, frustration, and conflict, which are there to encourage our development.

---

*This does not imply that the sign placements of planets present problems in themselves. The whole chart must be examined in each case.

The critic could point out that this concept of meaningful suffering and conflict leads to a laissez-faire attitude on the part of the individual, since neurosis would be warranted a place and a purpose in one's life. The eighteenth-century writer, Voltaire, in his novel *Candide*, satirized this attitude of clerics and philosophers toward the "higher purposes" of the sufferings and inequities of the world. "We live in the best of all possible worlds," he had his theologians blandly state. And, of course, astrology could be used to mystify real-life processes and thereby lead to a reluctance to change harmful societal attitudes and practices. My experience with astrologers, however, indicates that they are generally as concerned as educators and therapists with the need for healthier forms of living.

Objectivity

One end-product of the process of growing self-recognition, self-affirmation, and the sense of meaning that astrology can initiate is an increased objectivity. Astrologers Joan and Ken Negus describe the process: "Because the personality picture is on a piece of paper, the character becomes objectified, which gives the person a sense of security and detachment and therefore a sense of control. The murky depths become illumined."

Once we possess a more objective view of our character, life situation, and development, we can see where we can go realistically and what the impediments are to that forward movement. We then begin to gain a healthy feeling of control over our destiny, a sense of genuine power over our own lives, without which it is natural that we would be afraid to lose our neurotic controls and be unable to open up and discover our own unconscious processes.

This bears on the question of the necessary balance between subjectivity and objectivity, immersion and detachment. To live fully, we need to *experience* our lives—zestfully, with feeling, with our whole subjective being. At times life also demands that we stand back, become less immersed emotionally, and gain objectivity in order to find new direction. A healthy pulsation is is one of balance between these two aspects of functioning. Going to an astrologer is like receiving a dose of the medication called objectivity.

In the world of psychotherapy, psychoanalytic methods tend to overemphasize the mental examination of emotional and unconscious processes, to the neglect of the goal of real living through participation and immersion in emotionally-charged situations. The analytic patient frequently becomes too mental and objective, understanding the reasons and origins of behavior, but with a resultant loss of spontaneity and feeling. The more extreme emotional-cathartic therapies, such as primal therapy, on the other hand, tend to allow the loss of conscious, adult integration due to an excessive immersion in childhood emotional states. Psychotherapeutic methods are still emerging and still maturing, however. Ultimately, I believe we will see an integrated theory and technique whereby work on the conscious self and work on the unconscious self can take place simultaneously and be mutually nourishing and supportive.

Identification of Positive Potential

A particularly good use of astrology is its capacity to point out difficult aspects of an individual's personality and at the same time show the beneficial and constructive possibilities of these very traits. In astrology, any apparently negative aspect can become transformed into its more positive expression. A Moon-Venus opposition, for example, is not only an over-dependency on what others think of one and a tendency to please at any cost; it can, with work on the self, come to indicate graciousness and a sensitivity to others' needs. Astrology allows for *both*—nonjudgmentally—and it is this capacity that is one of its most healing properties. (This is not the same thing as the tendency of some astrologers to insist only on a kind of bland positivism. I discuss this problem on page 126.) Similarly, with a client with a Mars-square-Uranus that is not particularly offset by the rest of the chart, the astrologer will speak of the tendency to rash action, of course. But along with that, he or she can point out the stimulating energy the client has at his disposal for accomplishment and action once the poorly directed and rash impulses have been transformed.

Thus, in that very moment, the transformative process from destructive to positive will have begun: The client feels recognized even in his more difficult traits and therefore needs to hide and repress less; the client sees the destructive pattern more clearly and so begins to take control and responsibility for it; and finally, the client learns that even his most negative tendencies can become a source of positive power with time and effort.

What astrology suggests is that in each case there is a way through the fog, a potentially positive use and outcome of all human conditions. It is interesting to note that priests and ministers convey the same notion, the same implicit solace, but cannot back up their advice with anything specific about the individual the way the astrologer can. With them the moral pronouncement remains abstract and has no charge. Psychotherapy has to some extent inherited religion's old role; what used to be "sins" or "moral weaknesses" confessed to the priest are now one's "emotional problems." Unfortunately, a certain degree of negative judgment about psychological difficulties still persists in people's minds. Astrology avoids that dilemma and can participate in the transformative process freely, without having to overcome the person's fear of self-revelation.

Education in a Wisdom School

In reality, when a client who is "ready" seeks out an accomplished astrologer, it indicates a willingness to be educated by the teachings of an archetypal psychology, a "wisdom school," so to speak. The client—who now might be better termed "the student"—becomes sensitized to the nature of universal forces and principles and how they are manifesting in his or her psyche and life.

Where in our culture, our schools, or our psychotherapies, are we taught—as we are in astrology—about the painful but necessary growth experiences symbolized by the planet Saturn, as well as its useful focusing and concentrative functions? Where else do we learn about the contrasting energy of the planet Jupiter, with its offerings of ease, abundance, aspiration, and adventure, as well as the fact that even this expansive energy can be detrimental if it is not in balance with the rest of our needs? And where else do we learn of the different types of transformation expressed by Pluto, Uranus, and Neptune? Or that we all have the same essential qualities, needs, and opportunities (symbolized by the houses and signs) but with different emphasis and patterns and that one of our life tasks is to balance and harmonize these energies, even though they are sometimes polar opposites?

Learning about the significance of the planets, signs, houses, aspects, and cycles teaches us about the nature of the human condition. Astrology allows for the variety of individual temperament within universal law as no other system does. The different schemas of the psyche as described by Freud, Jung, and Reich are potent and valid; they should be thoroughly understood by astrologers for the enlargement of their vision and work, especially regarding repression, the unconscious, and the release of unconscious forces. What the horoscope provides that the great psychological teachers do not is an *immediate* overall picture of the patterns and textures of the individual personality, and through that a balanced and long-term view of how to work with that individual.

In the preceding discussion of some of the contributions and healing capacities of astrology, the picture I have drawn is of astrology at its best. Unfortunately, like any other medium for the advancement of people's psychological and spiritual development— including psychotherapy—astrology sometimes falls short of optimum effectiveness.

The reasons for the present failure of astrology to manifest

at a consistently high level are many, and some of them are not
well understood. Among these are the following:

- There is a lack of serious appreciation for the importance
  of astrological concepts in our culture, which even affects
  many of the very people who seek guidance from astrology.
- Many astrologers are at present insufficiently trained in
  the purely astrological procedures and technicalities used
  in their work.
- Most astrologers have little or no training in the concepts
  and techniques of counseling and scant knowledge of
  some of the basic theories of psychotherapy.
- Unresolved emotional and psychological problems on
  the part of the astrologer sometimes inhibit his or her
  effectiveness and interfere with the relationship with the
  client. (I treat this in detail in Chapters 9 and 12.)
- Whether they are aware of it or not, clients often harbor
  fear and a lack of readiness to examine wholeheartedly
  the significance of what a competent astrologer is actually describing.

It is ironic that similar difficulties are experienced in the
world of psychotherapy, except that psychotherapists and their
work are more highly regarded in our present-day world, where
medicine and statistical science reign supreme.

In the rest of this book I will be addressing issues of practical value to the astrologer, in particular the counseling role,
counseling techniques, and some of the specific psychodynamic
problems the astrologer is likely to encounter.

2

Psychological Dilemmas in the Practice of Astrology

Astrologers frequently find themselves confronted with difficulties in the course of their relationship with a client, and it is helfpul to know that many of these may be intrinsic to the role as it is now practiced. Psychotherapy, too, must deal with many of the same issues, the only difference being that psychotherapists are favored with greater social acceptance and have available to them training programs designed to resolve some of these problems. The point is that the dilemmas I am about to describe are inherent in the helping professions.

The Evocation of Therapy Needs

As previously stated, if the client is ready for honest self-appraisal and the astrological analysis is done competently, with no intrusion of unresolved aspects of the astrologer's personality, the client often feels deeply recognized and more conscious of her or his internal structure and potential. Yet, ironically, from this, its best quality—the ability to elucidate the depth psychology of a person in a qualitatively accurate way—there follows one of the major problems that astrologers must confront: the evocation of the client's need for a therapeutic relationship.

No doubt, an individual with a strong ego can use the heightened awareness astrology affords in her normal life development without any further assistance. But some people who see an astrologer come in distress, do not have a confident life adaptation, and either do not believe in psychotherapy or are currently involved in a therapy that is not helping them. What can, and does, happen is that the client will begin to reach out to the astrologer as a kind of friend, counselor, teacher, or therapist. The astrologer in turn might like the client, feel touched by his need for help, and begin to respond to requests for frequent consultations in person or by telephone. The question then arises as to how frequently the astrologer can see the client without developing a therapeutic relationship. What are the limits of astrological counseling? the responsibe astrologer asks. There are astrologers who draw the line at one visit a year, others at three or four times a year, whereas a few feel they can see a client as often as requested as long as the work seems to be of help, the client is not showing signs of serious psychopathology, and the astrologer is not taxed beyond the limits of energy and patience.

The picture becomes more complex, however, when a particular needy client reports progress for a while, becomes very involved in astrology, then grows dependent on the astrologer, and in time feels herself in a morass again. The astrologer is by then committed and in a predicament.

The fact is that astrology has an excellent body of knowledge for the beginning of genuine psychotherapy. What is missing, unfortunately, is the capacity to elicit the client's reactions in a continuing process that allows for the individual's development according to his or her own personal structure, life situation, and readiness to face unconscious forces.

Astrology has a great potential for stimulating further efforts at self-growth, including the search for a good psychotherapist. Indeed, it is difficult for me to conceive that a person of any intelligence and openness could hear himself described by a good astrologer and not feel recognized in a deep way and affirmed as an individual. Nonetheless, a person's deep fear of real change will resist this newly acquired self-knowledge, almost as much as another part of the total self will make efforts toward necessary change.

There arises from this, then, a corollary difficulty: how to guide the client to the healthy resolution of the conflicts astrology so accurately pinpoints. As Nancy Roof wrote in *Astrology Now* magazine:

> What astrologer has not experienced making a direct hit identifying the major psychological dynamics within his client and had his client not ask what could be done to resolve his conflict? Although no astrologer can presume to be a psychotherapist without training, he can offer suggestions or referrals. What he cannot do is leave the client hanging with the astrological knowledge but with no known means to solve the problem.[1]

A few astrologers are attempting to deal with this dilemma by taking graduate degrees in counseling and/or psychology. This is a difficult road to follow, however. First of all, it is extremely difficult to gain access to the few doctoral programs in clinical psychology that currently exist. Secondly, not many university counseling or psychology degrees offer the kind of training that would appeal to an astrologer. They often have a predominantly behaviorist or Freudian orientation and lack the humanistic, spiritual, and archetypal themes to which astrologers are drawn.

Another side to the dilemma of how or where to guide clients who want to explore themselves further is the fact that few astrologers have a working relationship with a competent psychotherapist who would be willing to accept the astrologer's interpretations or even be open to referrals. Astrologers will always be in a position to encounter some client who shows evidence of serious emotional problems that the astrologer knows is beyond his or her domain. The best thing the astrologer can do in that case is to suggest that the client find a therapist. Yet the client, who must respect the astrologer to some degree if he has been brought to this point, would feel more comfortable with a therapist whom the astrologer could recom-

---

[1] Nancy Roof, "Dilemmas of Astrology," *Astrology Now*, no. 23 (November 1978–January 1979), p. 19.

mend. There is a great need for the opening up of professional channels between astrologers and psychotherapists, and I can only hope that this book will help in the progress toward that end.

Expectations of Magic

There is a general human tendency to look for immediate and magical solutions to complex life questions, and this presents another persistent difficulty inherent in the astrologer-client relationship. For astrology provides an optimum situation for the satisfaction of this unrealistic wish, since it affords genuine knowledge about a person from apparently mysterious sources and without effort on the part of the client.

For those clients who have a tendency to place responsibility for their problems on external influences, astrology unfortunately provides ample opportunity for the development of excessive dependency. Even when the astrologer himself does not have such a deterministic or passive philosophy, astrology and the astrologer can seem like oracles to the client. Indeed, latent infantile strivings to be taken care of by an all-knowing parent can easily be triggered off. (I deal with this dilemma at greater length in Chapter 9.) In this regard, Stephen Arroyo, in *Astrology, Psychology, and the Four Elements,* wrote:

> However, one [the astrologer] should realize that merely giving advice without also giving a means of deeper understanding is of little value, for each person must do his or her own work and must, through his or her own experience, arrive at the higher awareness that enables the person to outgrow or transcend the difficulty.[2]

---

[2] Stephen Arroyo, *Astrology, Psychology, and the Four Elements* (Reno, Nevada: CRCS Publications, 1975), p. 52. Available from the publisher of this book.

Belief in the Omniscience of the Astrologer

If astrological clients have a tendency to see the astrologer as holding the key to the mystery of the inner life and the future, what must this do to the astrologer's personal sense of power and importance?

As an astrologer friend, Jeff Jawer, wrote to me,

> It is extremely frustrating that astrology has so much to offer, yet is so thoroughly disregarded by the general public and by the therapeutic community. I feel certain that the power of astrology intimidates some professionals, who are locked into their own perspectives on healing. Some highly intelligent and educated individuals I know have avoided studying astrology for fear that it will present them with a world view too inclusive for them. But as any student of astrology learns, the subject is quite open-ended, with much room for individual expression, interpretation, and application. Astrologers, I am sure, are partly to blame. It is difficult to reject the image of the all-seeing, all-knowing sage. I myself was attracted to astrology for the powerful insights it can generate. Such an elevated position of special knowledge can be very appealing. I am sure that there have been studies made of the type of person who becomes a therapist that would apply to astrologers as well.

My correspondent is correct in his assumption that power issues and unresolved ego drives are also to be found in the therapeutic community. Adolph Guggenbohl-Craig, a Swiss Jungian analyst, has written about this in clear and strong language.[3] There is always the possibility, indeed the inevitability, of ego problems being acted out by persons in a position of authority in the healing arts. Neither doctor, therapist, astrologer, psychic, nor spiritual counselor is exempt.

The temptation to "play God" is strong for some astrologers, since the astrological information contains such powerful

---

[3] See Adolph Guggenbohl-Craig, *Power in the Helping Professions* (New York: Spring Publications, 1971). Available from the publisher of this book.

insights, so many clients are needy and arrive with great expectations, and some even demand this kind of magical power from the "all-knowing" astrologer. (This problem is discussed in Chapter 12.) The majority of astrologers, however, are aware of their position of responsibility and authority and the resulting need for them to be conscious and act with conscience.

Cloaking Oneself in Astrology

One of the more complex dilemmas in astrology is the tendency of many people who are especially enthusiastic about the work to see too much of their lives in astrological terms. It reminds me of followers of orthodox psychoanalysis, who view every act, every word, and every gesture as being caused by some hidden neurotic need. In both cases, the construct functions as a belief system that provides a basis of orientation and security but in truth limits one's vision.

If, as I have said, the astrological symbology provides the widest, as well as the most individualized, psychologically valid descriptive system in existence, and through it a person is enabled to feel uniquely affirmed and in harmony with universal patterns of existence, what then is the drawback in using astrological understanding extensively? Can it ever be used too much?

Let us look at it this way: The objectivity and detachment about experiences that astrological understanding gives results in a feeling of control. It enables us to disengage ourselves from emotionally charged situations. For example, a person can say that he acted in a fickle manner because his Sun is in Gemini. If he is not an inwardly responsible person, he can use the Gemini label as an excuse for his behavior. A more serious Gemini will view the behavior as one of the more negative features of his Gemini ego that needs correction. The point is that in either case the explanation derived from the fact of one's being a Gemini provides a degree of security in respect to the behavior. By contrast, the person who acts fickly but does not explain it astrologically will feel more of a need to answer for that kind of behavior, both to himself and to others. In a word, a negative feature of astrology that we in astrological circles need to face is that it can be used as a protective device as well as a liberating one.

Astrology can be used as a "cloak" in two other ways, both of them well known: in the beginning stages of relationships and for predicting the future. There are people who will not venture into a possible relationship with a person unless they know his or her chart. Others will not make any decision in life without knowing the transiting conditions. In both situations there is a definite implicit statement that the person does not have the confidence to enter into any new experience with only his or her own knowledge of life, thoughts, perceptions, and feelings for a guide. One is saying that one doesn't feel mature enough, perceptive enough, confident enough to venture into life with just oneself.

In the last chapter, I noted that astrological understanding can give a person wisdom and objectivity about the self to work more effectively for self-transformation. This is certainly true. But even the finest of systems can be misused and can never be made to cover all aspects of experience. Fundamentally, in order to grow we all have to learn to face life situations unaided except for our own perceptions, desires, judgments, and beliefs. Consulting an astrologer about every important situation in life can interfere with that necessary growth.

3

The Astrologer's Confusing Role

Almost all of the astrologers I know, except for those who are strictly involved in research, call themselves astrological counselors. Yet this term covers such a wide range of practices that it is in fact misleading. There is a great difference between the one-time consultation, in which the astrologer does 98 percent of the talking, and the development of an interpersonal relationship between astrologer and client, with fairly frequent visits over a period of time and the involvement of a much larger part of the client's personality. Astrologers function at both ends of the spectrum and all gradations in between. The latter situation, in which a genuine relationship is allowed to develop, possesses some of the qualities of psychotherapy and counseling, whereas the one-time consultation involves the simple passing on of information and is similar to what we think of traditionally as education. (Chapter 4, "The Three Forms of Astrology," goes into this extensively.)

Let us define, first, the difference between education, counseling, and psychotherapy within the context of the helping/healing arts. Although there is no sharp demarcation between the three disciplines, the differences in technique, involvement, and responsibility are significant. All three forms can be therapeutic, depending on the readiness and receptivity of the client. But what do we mean by the term *therapeutic*? Any activity that enhances the growth, awareness, productivity, aliveness, or wholeness of a person is therapeutic.

Education, in the traditional sense (as opposed to the ideal sense), refers to a process in which a person obtains information, knowledge, or technique from someone else who already possesses it. It is essentially one-directional and can vary from a tedious rote-learning to an inspirational opening up of intellectual horizons and consciousness. Many first-time astrological consultations have this educational quality but range considerably from the didactic to the truly enlightening. The client isn't sure what he or she is looking for, passively listens, perhaps occasionally comments or asks questions. The individual may come away with merely a superficial, intellectual acceptance of the idea that astrology "makes some sense," may manage to remember a few terms and generalizations, and then do nothing more than file the horoscope away in a bottom drawer. Alternatively, the reading may effect a deep and stirring realization, which results in the nascent acceptance of one's character and struggles and the impetus to further growth and work on the self. Out of this may arise a whole new dimension of meaning and purpose to life. This latter is very therapeutic indeed.

The astrological consultation takes on more of the qualities of counseling when the client enters into the interpersonal exchange with questions and responses or when the consultation begins with the client's request for clarity about a specific life problem and the natal chart and current transits are examined with that in mind. In general, the more the astrologer and client engage in dialogue, the closer the relationship approaches to a counseling situation.

It is important to note that there is potentially a large difference between astrological counseling and nonastrological counseling. When the client comes to the astrologer, the implicit question the client asks is "What can you tell me about myself?" But when the client comes to the counselor, the direction of flow is reversed; it is the counselor who asks the client, "What is your problem? Tell me about yourself." The astrological counselor feeds information, wisdom, and guidance to a largely inactive participant. The nonastrological counselor

attempts to draw out hidden areas of knowledge and drive, with
the goal of activating the client.

However, the fact is that both possibilities are available to
the astrologer, and it is around exactly this point, I believe, that
the astrologer becomes confused. As an astrologer begins to see
a client on a continuing basis, the need develops to bring into
the counseling situation some of the facts of the person's present life, attitudes, and emotional states so that the current
transits can be rendered more meaningful. In addition, guiding
the client to new behaviors and attitudes requires some knowledge of the technique of personality investigation and exchange,
the psychodynamics of transference, the principles of intrapsychic conflict, and so on. As some astrologers have complained to me, "We can see the problem so well, but once we
have identified it, what do we do about it?"

This leads us to the need to differentiate between nonastrological counseling and psychotherapy. The basic difference
in practice is that psychotherapy is long-term and intense and
aims not only at improving the immediate life problems and
helping the person actualize his or her potential, but also at
psychological change on a deep level. Counseling, on the other
hand, is briefer and usually aimed at specific problem areas,
such as marital discord or career difficulty. The discussion will
usually center around some of the underlying attitudes and
needs of the client that require clarification, but the effort at
depth-psychological change* will not be made. All in all, there
will be less of a relationship, in contrast to the ongoing relationship that develops in psychotherapy. Consequently, there will
be less possibility for dependency, transference, and countertransference to occur. Defenses will usually be challenged less
in counseling, or not at all, and emotions and images will not
be consciously evoked. The work is more on the conscious
aspects of the personality as perceived by the individual. The

---

*This refers to the serious modification of long-term habits and atti-
tudes that involve the whole person, such as marked shyness, arrogance,
flippancy, and so on.

psychotherapy patient, by contrast, comes to the situation feeling much more troubled by his or her habitual patterns and is therefore willing to work through the more painful process of internal change. In the broadest sense, psychotherapy is the attempt to change a person's internal structure, whereas counseling is the attempt to help an individual deal more effectively with immediate problems without requiring significant internal change. Nevertheless, there is a gradual area of transition between the two where the boundaries are blurred.

It is important for astrologers to ask themselves whether they are offering an educational service or whether they are in fact practicing counseling or aspects of psychotherapy. The amount of involvement with the client in terms of both time and emotional demands, the need for skills of therapeutic intervention, and the degree of responsibility for one's effect on a person's life are intensified as one proceeds in the direction from education to counseling to psychotherapy.

Such a breakdown as the one I have just made is valuable for the purposes of simplification and clarification, but it is also necessary to remember that because of the nature of astrology, even the one-time astrological consultation with minimal client participation is not entirely a merely educational process. Many clients come to the consultation in a state of significant personal distress and may arrive full of hope and faith in the ability of the astrologer to heal. Under these circumstances, every utterance of the astrologer, whether it be supportive or able to be interpreted as criticism, has the potential of being significantly helpful or deleterious. Therefore, even astrological education has within it the seed for a beginning in-depth psychotherapy, since it deals with character structure in a deep and valid way. In general, my impression is that many astrologers function, without realizing it, partly as in-depth psychological educators, partly as counselors, and to a certain extent as psychotherapists.

The educational aspect will always be essential to all types of astrological consultation, because the knowledge gained from the horoscope, of which the astrologer is the expert interpreter, is basic to the transaction. But as the astrologer enters more and more into the immediate and ongoing growth and transformative processes of the client, the quality of the work changes. The extent to which astrologers feel themselves to be educators on the one hand, healers on the other, varies considerably. For example, Michael and Margaret Erlewine, in an article entitled "The Counselor: Midwife of the Psyche" in *Astrology Now*, wrote:

> In trying to think of a way to communicate what does happen in the counseling process, we came upon what is an almost perfect analogy—the midwife. The function of the midwife is to assist both the mother and the child through the birth process. Her entire role is to facilitate a process that is already unfolding rather than to initiate or do anything herself. The counselor or reader also functions as a midwife, a midwife of the psyche or soul, a midwife of the spirit. It is not the function of the astrologer-counselor to imbue or fill the client with knowledge, facts, or direction. Instead, the counselor, like the midwife, can but assist in the unfoldment of the natural process.[4]

Some astrologers, because of their innate sensitivity and therapeutic capacity, their real desire to serve, and the rich life experience they have to draw upon, allow themselves to become involved in frequent consultations with a client who is very needy and at the same time resistant to psychotherapy. A classic, implicitly psychotherapeutic situation develops based on a special triad: the neediness of the client, the readiness to serve on the part of the astrologer, and a unique body of knowledge that gives both parties a feeling of some security and purpose. Out of this arises some of the major challenges astrology must confront. One is that the excellent psychological analysis provided by the astrological reading not infrequently stimulates the need for further in-depth psychological efforts. If the client is already involved in a good psychotherapeutic process, it only

---

[4] Michael and Margaret Erlewine, "The Counselor: Midwife of the Psyche," *Astrology Now*, no. 23 (November 1978–January 1979), p. 26.

aids that process. If the client is not in therapy but has a strong ego, then astrology aids in further growth and life enhancement. But if the client is particularly needy and has a "shaky" ego, if the client is fearful of psychotherapy or is not benefiting from the psychotherapy he or she is engaged in, there develops the real need for a therapy transaction with the astrologer. After all, the client realizes, the astrologer seems better able even than the psychotherapist to recognize her or his unique psychological makeup, since the psychotherapist tends to interpret all of life and the individual himself in terms of a particular psychological theory.

A second major challenge grows from the first: the need to proceed from the description and understanding of a person's conflicts to some way of practically assisting in the resolution of those conflicts. ("We see the problem so well, but what to do about it!")

Take, for example, a client who has Mars in Aries square Saturn in Cancer. Let us say there is a good deal of Fire and cardinality in the chart, but there are also other natal configurations besides the Saturn-square-Mars that indicate a fear of assertion and action. The astrologer might begin by encouraging the client to look for more creative outlets for her blocked energy, since fine communicative skills are indicated by the chart's strong third-house/ninth-house axis. A good beginning, certainly. But this client is already teaching in a university setting in a field she wholeheartedly embraces. Yet she still feels blocked about being able to reach some deep source of her creative potential.

Perhaps the astrologer senses a good deal of body tension in the woman and recommends procedures to relieve it, such as massage, dance movement, swimming, or running. These help, but permanent body loosening cannot occur until character structure and attitudes begin to be worked with consciously and the underlying emotions are released and genuine insights developed.

A more adventurous or therapeutically inclined astrologer might recommend individual and/or group therapy to get in touch with the anger and to let go of the ego controls. But let us say that in this particular client there is also an emphasis on Scorpio or Pluto. Is it possible that by supporting the client's aggressiveness, the newly opened power will be used to dominate and manipulate rather than for the development of a healthy capacity for appropriate anger?

There are so many potentials in any given chart, how is the astrologer to know which potential needs to emerge next in the client's life? The answer lies in the astrologer's ability to explore and assess the client's *present* life functioning and needs. It is commonly said that astrology is a road map, not the countryside itself. If the astrologer is to apply the road-map information correctly, then there is a need to explore what the person has done and is doing with that psychological potential.

Let us go further with our hypothetical client's problem with her Mars energy (ego assertion, the ability to take action, potential for anger, sexuality). Besides relating the problem to the chart as a whole and to the transits, progressions, and so on, in order to counsel such a client effectively one should also know something about the following:

- The client's present ego state, or self-image
- The client's fantasies and images of assertive action, as well as the feared consequences of same
- The client's previous experience with assertion
- What role the client generally adopts as a defense against assertiveness (for example, the "nice person" role, the "professorial" role, the distant, detached attitude, and so on)
- How the parents were seen to express their Mars energy
- The present status and history of the emotional life: whether the client has experienced anxiety, depression, tendencies to rage, and so on
- Whether the client regularly has dreams that express aggression
- The kind of body language exhibited during the consul-

tation that might indicate the degree of internal tension, subtle expressions of hostility, suspiciousness, or submissiveness

Knowledge of even a few of these aspects could indicate to what extent the client could be expected to take new action and in what areas. For example, if the astrologer can ascertain that the client's work and social life are fairly active and that she does not experience extended periods of anxiety and/or depression, then he can feel justified in supporting more intense movements toward change and action than he can with a person whose work and social functioning appear more troubled. Or, if the client has a particularly shy and demure personality, the astrologer could assume with confidence that she was internally very threatened by strong assertive action and anger. The astrologer would therefore need to gently explore the client's fears and fantasies about her Mars energies in order to desensitize her a little from the fear of them. He could then discuss some new ways of action and assertion that the client had fantasized about but dismissed, at the same time bringing in other aspects of the natal potential that might be applicable.

If the astrologer were to explore only a few of these areas of the client's psychological life, he would be doing real counseling and beginning psychotherapy. However, this can be unsteady ground for even the most experienced and astute of astrologers. It is for this reason I believe that astrologers should augment their astrological knowledge with counseling and psychology courses and, if possible, special training. I would also recommend that the astrologer consider getting some psychotherapy himself.

Finally, the reader may ask, if astrologers take courses in counseling and psychology or get postgraduate degrees, won't they tend to lose their identity as astrologers, becoming neither fish nor fowl? The answer is no. Modern-day rational "scientism" cannot destroy the ancient wisdom of astrology. But a new species of healer might arise, one who can combine the archetypal, symbolic knowledge of astrology with some of the valid concepts and techniques from modern psychological therapies.

4

The Three Forms of Astrology

I have made reference to three different levels of astrological work with clients: astrological education, astrological counseling, and astro-therapy. In this chapter I will discuss these three functions in greater detail in terms of their differing psychological effects on clients and the varying degrees of training required of the astrologers who practice them.

The form of astrology that any particular astrologer practices will vary according to his or her interests, temperament, training, and feeling of readiness, as well as the immediate need of the client. It is probably rare that an astrologer subscribes to one form only, since what distinguishes them from each other is basically a matter of emphasis. Most astrologers are probably educators and do a minimal degree of counseling. A minority of astrologers would emphasize the counseling quality of their work over the educational aspects. Astro-therapy is rare, I believe.

All three forms can be helpful, though each also has its limitations. All three possess a therapeutic dimension, even astrological education. The horoscope, if competently interpreted, sheds light on the depth psychology of a person and can open consciousness to an awareness of the self, which is an aspect of any real therapeutic process. There are some distinctions that can be made between the three forms, however.

Astrological Education

What I call astrological education is what commonly goes by the term *chart reading*. It essentially consists of *providing information* of a general kind.

The astrologer "reads," or interprets, the horoscope, transits, and progressions to a largely nonparticipating individual. There is little or no dialogue, and only a small cross-section of the client's present life, problems, and attitudes is elicited or discussed. Sometimes a minimal degree of counseling occurs when the client mentions a current life problem in passing and the astrologer attempts to place this problem within the context of the overall interpretation, but the problem is not explored to any significant extent.

I know several astrologers who consider this approach to be largely a waste of time—at best. They feel it appeals to the need some astrologers have to inflate their own egos by playing power games at the expense of the client. The obvious danger of such an approach is that it can render the client passive, and dependent on external sources of self-knowledge.

All of this notwithstanding, the fact of the matter is that many astrologers are invariably called upon to do a certain percentage of their consultations from an educational point of view. For many clients, this is their first exposure to the kind of psychological overview astrology has to offer, and they will naturally be testing in their minds the possible validity or invalidity of this unconventional approach. Understandably, such a client is not willing to trust a stranger, and an unknown interpretive method with a revelation of serious life problems and internal states.

Furthermore, if the astrologer does not have another source of income, she or he is dependent on the clients who ask for consultations and must adapt to their needs, even if these preclude a real interchange. In addition, the astrologer, called upon to demonstrate the powers of this ancient and esoteric science, feels compelled to examine the complexity of the horoscope thoroughly, which may leave little time for feedback from the client. All in all, it is a potentially power-laden situation and presents a true challenge to the modern explorer of the soul.

Given these inevitable preconditions, how much therapeutic value can astrological education be said to have? I have already spoken of the positive effect *any* astrological information can have when the client is a searching individual. Astrological education can enable the client to get an excellent overview of his or her psychological structure, with consequent growth in self-recognition, self-validation, and self-acceptance. Both the beginning of a deeper search into the self and a sense of life's purpose can be stimulated. With this understood, therefore, let us look more closely at the difficulties that are inherent in this form of astrology.

Limited Client Response

A principal drawback of the astrological reading is the necessary condition of minimal client participation. For one thing, without some client response, the astrologer is forced into the role of a performer. Conveyor of an "unquestionable source of knowledge," she or he bears the burden of being implicitly expected to succeed completely in convincing the client of its validity; and it is certainly possible that the astrologer does not know whether the reading has rendered only an approximate or qualified description of the client's personality.

Take the case of a male client with the Moon in a Water sign in hard aspect to Uranus, and with Neptune in the first house. The astrologer will conclude that this person has a tendency to intense emotional reactions and is inclined to be oversusceptible to stress and conflict. (She will then go on to examine the rest of the chart for other natal configurations that would reinforce the emotional instability, as well as potentials that would counterbalance this, such as an emphasis on Earth signs or a strong Saturn or Sun.) In this hypothetical situation, after the astrologer has commented briefly on the emotional picture, the client relates that he has a short fuse on his temper but then quickly fears rejection or has guilt feelings. The client might ask for clarification of his emotional "problem." The astrologer, in turn, has some concern of her own about loss of emotional control (see page 116) and has ambivalent opinions about the practicality of how to resolve such depth problems. Furthermore, if she is to give a comprehensive reading, not much time is allotted for exploring any particular aspect of the client's chart. Her response to the client is to suggest that he think about new ways to handle his emotions rather than through losing his temper so easily and that perhaps if he felt more accomplishment in his work life, he would be less temperamental. The client feels that the astrologer is generally correct, but doesn't really know what to do with the advice.

The point here is that the client cannot receive the fullest benefit that the astrological information can provide in a chart reading alone. Only if the prospective client is genuinely unwilling to share any of her or his concerns, problems, and present life is the reading the most appropriate and helpful mode of astrological understanding. The reason for this is that without the possibility of real dialogue with the client, the astrologer is on unsteady ground in regard to the discussion of problematic areas of the horoscope. The astrologer could tell a female client with Venus in hard aspect to Saturn, for example, "You have fear or self-doubt in the love area of your life." The client might appear nonchalant or unaffected but could carry away the feeling that there is something terribly wrong with her ability to express love. This kind of reaction would be especially likely if the client has found the reading impressive in other respects or if the astrologer speaks with authority and doesn't consciously look for client response.

I know at least one astrologer who is careful to avoid this problem by asking clients how they experience the pattern she describes to them. She also precedes the reading by specifically encouraging the client to ask questions or give responses anytime during the consultation. Alternatively, some astrologers think it wise simply to back away from the painful subject if they detect an uncomfortable reaction on the part of the client.

Victimization and Dependency

For some people the astrological reading can be valuable in reducing guilt and self-doubt, providing a sense of meaning and order in their life. Yet, for others, it tends to foster the feeling that they are the passive victim of fate. The very nature of the consultation is conducive to this kind of attitude because of the fact that the client is basically inactive and nonparticipating throughout the reading.

Now, if added to this general climate, you have a client who comes to the reading full of self-doubt and without direction and an astrologer who presents his or her interpretation of the chart in a strong Saturnian, parental manner, you have the ingredients for a possible chronic dependent attitude developing in the client. It is all too easy to blame the planets or feel oneself the passive recipient of their energies. Astrologers continually tell their students that the planets don't compel people's behavior, yet the inclination toward this belief is present in more than a few.

It should be realized that the responsibility for this attitude is not predominantly that of the astrologer. People who are inclined to view astrology this way would likely do the same with another system. However, some astrologers add to the problem by attempting to be too impressive or certain of their knowledge and by failing to recognize the signs of dependency or victimization when they occur.

Intrusion of the Astrologer

Since the client gets to express himself only minimally in the reading, a vacuum is created whereby aspects of the astrologer's own personality difficulties can intrude. The more mature and responsible professionals are acutely aware of this potential and try to be conscious to keep watch over their own egos, overambitiousness, and inner conflicts.

One experienced astrologer I know does a synastry analysis of the relationship between herself and prospective clients, and if her Neptune is on a personal planet of the client's, she refers the person to another astrologer. Although this degree of conservatism may not be necessary for most astrologers, it does suggest the seriousness of the problem.

The only way the astrologer can keep in touch with the client during a reading is by periodically eliciting the client's responses to the interpretations. This serves two important purposes. First, the client is far less likely to walk away from the consultation in a self-critical state. And second, by observing his or her conjectures reflected in a living way, the astrologer learns and grows.

Astrological Counseling

Although it must, by its very nature, still provide a good amount of information to the client, astrological counseling also involves a *dialogue* with the person in order to aid him or her in the working out of current life problems. The astrological information is geared toward the conscious and verbalized concerns of the client—his or her present life, problems, attitudes, and needs—and the individual is no longer a quiet student-listener but a more active participant.

The conditions under which astrological counseling can occur are many. It may be fair to apply the term to a one-time consultation if the client requests a definite focus on the solving of a life problem or reveals significant aspects of her or his internal life to the astrologer. Counseling also typically occurs when the client sees the astrologer more than once a year, since the client usually reveals personal need in this situation. Furthermore, the proper interpretation of such ephemeral conditions as transits, solar returns, and so on virtually compel the astrologer to inquire about the person's life in order to be better able to orient that person to their meanings and opportunities.

Advantages of Counseling

In astrological counseling work, astrologers have the opportunity to render the information more personal and practical than in a simple reading. They are able to deepen and focus the material to meet the present needs of the individual. Having a more definite idea of what a person has made of his or her potential, the astrologer can interpret with greater precision the present meaning and function of astrological aspects, configurations, and the possible effects of transits. No longer is the astrologer simply interpreting symbols on a piece of paper; he or she is interacting with a sensitive human being in need. Here is where astrology becomes a living reality.

Gina Ceaglio, in an article in *Astrology Now*, wrote,

> For myself, I have outlined a very short fact-sheet that is filled out for every consultation. In addition to the vital statistics, it covers profession, marital status (or live-in arrangement), children and their ages, referral source, and, most important of all, the area of life that is presently of greatest concern. To be sure, when I set up the chart and progress it, I will recognize where the innate discomforts are felt and where the current concentration is focused. *However, I believe it is essential to productive counseling to have the client's view of his own problem area* [italics mine].[5]

Another method would be to explore the needs, problems, and life circumstances of the person during the first part of the consultation.

A client with Venus square Saturn, for example, could react in diverse ways to this aspect of inhibition and self-doubt about the ability to relate to others and express love needs. The person might remain basically shy and isolated in love relationships, overcompensate for the self-doubt with excessive sexual openness, hold on desperately to a minimally satisfying relationship, or become hypercritical of others as a projection of self-criticism. Once the astrologer has not only the background knowledge of the total horoscope, progressions, and transits, but also the additional information about the client's life that only the client can reveal, he or she is in a stronger position to

---

[5] Gina Ceaglio, "Creative Focus," *Astrology Now,* no 23 (November 1978–January 1979), p. 22.

counsel the person regarding this aspect. Real dialogue is a pre-requisite of good counseling, for it stimulates the client to respond to unclarified and difficult ideas. In such a climate the astrologer is better able to prevent the possibility that the client will leave the consultation with a negative feeling about himself due to a discussion of a vulnerable aspect of his personality.

Impact of the Counselor's Personality

Since counseling involves the dynamic interaction of helper and seeker, the counselor will be called upon to express her or his personality and inner state considerably more than in a reading. If the astrologer doesn't know himself in a deep emotional way and has significant psychological defenses, then he will have difficulty perceiving, interpreting, and handling the reactions of the client. The astrologer who has a particular fear of anger and confrontation, for instance, will feel awkward or upset with a hostile client, whereas an astrologer who is not personally threatened by this will spontaneously know what to do in most situations of this kind. I cannot emphasize enough that astrologers who contemplate doing frequent counseling first examine themselves for their degree of maturity and consider enbarking upon a period of therapy themselves as well as getting some training in counseling and/or psychology.

Challenges in the Dialogue

Entering into a counseling situation means the significant inclusion of the present life and psychic content of the client. No longer is the existence of the astrological material as a major focus enough. Now the astrologer needs a good ability in the art of dialogue and psychological exploration. He or she must be able to draw out the client. The verbal exchange between counselor and client becomes the fulcrum, as it is in nonastrological counseling.

Much has been written in books on counseling about the proper way to conduct a dialogue for the purposes of exploration: The ability to listen well, an empathetic and genuine manner, simple and appropriate questions, and a real understanding of what the client is trying to say are all important. This is as appropriate for the astrologer as it is for the non-astrological counselor.

The astrologer must be especially watchful for the possibility that she or he will make too-rapid conclusions about the client's present life and problems from the astrological material or will guide the questioning from those assumptions exclusively. It is true that with the application to the natal chart of transits and progressions, the astrologer usually has a fairly good idea of the issues occurring in the client's present life. With that well-established beginning, the astrologer necessarily directs her major thrust of inquiry along these lines. This is, of course, appropriate counseling procedure. The problem is that too much confidence in her prior knowledge of the client can lead the astrologer to focus only on those issues of concern to her—to the neglect of other real concerns of the client. The astrologer must clearly understand that difficulties and questions of the client that are outside of the main thesis of the astrologer can give valuable insights and can amplify what the astrologer already predicts and perceives.

For example, a man comes to an astrologer with the fear that he is about to lose a serious love relationship. The astrological data indicate that transiting Pluto is exactly conjunct the client's Neptune in the seventh house. Natally the man has Venus in Pisces and no Earth in his chart. The astrologer concludes that the client is facing the loss of an ideal romantic image in partners in a love relationship and pursues this line of observation and questioning. Undoubtedly, this is a deep psychological pressure on the client in the present circumstances, but possibly on an unconscious level. What this individual is most concerned about, on a conscious level, is his fear of loss, failure, and pain. By neglecting the more conscious issues of the client for what the transit and horoscope indicate, the astrologer is denying immediate help to the client. The loss of a romantic ideal can be talked about from the educational perspective, that is, its meaning can be understood in the broadest sense, but if the client responds in a limited way because of his lack of emotional readiness to deal with this issue, then his needs of the moment should be the first order of business.

Astro-Therapy

In astrological therapy the astrologer *participates in a regular, ongoing way in the depth-psychological change of the individual.* Here the transformative process is consciously worked at, so that the astrologer now faces issues of dependency and transference in an intense, emotional relationship. The astrologer's practical knowledge must now include areas that supercede astrology itself, such as training in aspects of psychodynamics, the analysis of character structure, and the subtleties of working with defenses and unconscious forces. (See Chapters 6 and 7.)

The astrologer goes beyond providing occasional guidelines for change, as in counseling; he or she now becomes an active participant in that change. In astrological education, the patterns of psychological structure and process are revealed, and this often opens the door to fuller consciousness of the real self, making it, in effect, the first step in the "therapy of life."* This essential change in understanding is not the same thing, however, as the necessary working out of conflicts, blocks, and imbalances. So that if the reading can be thought of as a beacon light, astrological counseling takes it one step further, for here the astrologer becomes a moderately active helper in the process of change. Finally, with astro-therapy, the astrologer assumes the task of full-time sharer and guide.

What is the basis of the transition from astrological counseling to astro-therapy? Many experienced astrologers believe that the counseling takes on a therapy function when the client sees

---

*By the "therapy of life" I mean the emotional and spiritual growth people can experience simply by dealing with life's demands and opportunities directly.

the astrologer regularly, as often as once a month. In this case, more than astrological information has to be utilized, and a clearly dependent and transferential relationship develops.

The relationship can turn into astro-therapy even when the client sees the astrologer less often than monthly. This happens when the astrologer, ignoring the demonstrated resistances and vulnerabilities of the client, feels obliged to reveal the murky, unresolved aspects of the person's psyche no matter what and pushes for a too-rapid or too-deep change. This would be, clearly, a rather aggressive, nonhelpful form of astro-therapy.

Some astrologers, however, have a natural gift for doing therapy. Their years of experience as an astrological counselor have given them a real training in the dynamics of the life process and human psyche. The horoscope provides a potent means of diagnosing and understanding the individual. Furthermore, many people come to astrologers seeking a kind of halfway house of therapy. Being a sensitive and concerned person, the astrologer finds the temptation to venture into the domain of astro-therapy great.

Astrologers should know that there are many potential risks involved in astro-therapy as well as productive uses. There are more demands on the astrologer as a result of the increased emotional charge; there's a greater need for knowledge of technique; and the degree of personal responsibility is increased. Even with a highly sensitive astrologer who has a rich and mature life experience, there is a definite need for additional training and therapy experience if she or he is to undertake such work. Any practitioner in this field must have an appreciation and knowledge of the following.

- Methods for loosening the defenses
- How to work with repressed emotions, needs, and archetypal forces once they begin to be expressed
- Techniques for working with the imagination, fantasies, and dreams
- Theories of psychodynamics, psychopathology, and character types beyond what astrology has to offer

- How to work with transference and countertransference problems
- How to foster the growth of a good self-concept
- Theories of the individual within the total life context, including the familial, social, and business or professional milieu.

As astrologers gain experience in working with clients over the course of time, they need to enlarge and deepen their knowledge of how astrology can best be applied to the various circumstances with which they are called upon to deal. In order to gain increased self-awareness, they can ask themselves various questions regarding the educational, counseling, and therapeutic aspects of their work. Though not always answerable, some of the following questions may be of benefit:

- What is the client really looking for?
- What is the client ready to hear?
- Why is the client coming to see me at this point in his or her life?
- What is the best way to use the astrological information to help the client develop her or his sense of initiative, responsibility, and participation in life?
- What is the appropriate kind and degree of exploration to be done of this client's life and psyche?
- Does the client really need psychotherapy? If so, what is the appropriate way of offering that opinion?
- Does the client challenge any sore spots of my own?
- What are my strengths and weaknesses as an astrologer?
- Am I a teacher, counselor, or therapist? What is it I'm really doing?
- Am I expecting that I will be able to change this client's life? Is this expectation realizable? Am I looking for too-rapid change?

5

The Growth of Astrology as a Psychological Tool

That astrological counseling is not completely separate from the mental health field is evident for several reasons: More than a few astrologers are studying counseling and psychology in graduate schools across the country; many modern psychological terms that are of a nonastrological origin are used by astrologers in their readings and lectures, terms such as *ego, superego, projection, identification, unconscious,* and so on; astrologers face situations in which they must be able to assess serious emotional conditions in a client and refer that person to another form of healing; a greater proportion of the general public is beginning to take astrology seriously and to place it in context with the other accepted philosophies and psychologies; some astrologers are beginning to work with psychotherapists.

There is a need for growth in every discipline if rigidity and narrow-mindedness are not to set in. It is my view that astrology can grow along four different but related routes: (a) the scientific research of people such as the Gauquelins and others; (b) the depth-psychological orientation of astrologers such as Stephen Arroyo, Liz Greene, Robert Hand, Richard Idemon, and others; (c) the availability of comprehensive astrological teaching programs; and (d) the assimilation of theory and technique from nonastrological counseling and psychotherapy. It is this last area that we are concerned with in this book. (Of course, another volume could, and should, be written about the other side of the coin the ways in which psychotherapy and counseling can benefit from astrology.)

The need for such cross-fertilization is obvious. Both forms of counseling—astrological and nonastrological—have something the other lacks. Astrological counseling provides a symbolic framework for understanding the basic psychological patterns of the individual, as well as the cycles of development the person has to undergo. Such an overall picture helps in that it gives perspective and self-knowledge in tackling the struggle of life. But what astrology lacks is a set of specific techniques to help people work out the conflicts and problems it so clearly describes. Nonastrological counseling, by contrast, has mainly the living interaction between client and counselor to work with. Because of this, the counselor must be adept at using effective exploratory and interview techniques. The nonastrological counselor is trained to look for the immediate need and emotional capacity of the client; the underlying conflicts, motivations, blocks, and confused defenses and roles; the interactional dynamics between counselor and client; and the basic self-concept as it relates to the total life situation of the client.

These and other counseling methods could be learned to some degree in a good counseling or psychology course. How would this serve the astrologer? First, by the use of some initial exploration of the life and attitudes of the client prior to the astrological part of the consultation, the astrologer would be better able to assess the client's needs. This, in turn, would stimulate the client's participation during the reading, thus making the exchange more dynamic, more alive, and potentially more helpful.

Then, in follow-up consultations, the astrologer would have some practical ways of helping the client work out the complexities and stresses that are revealed in the natal chart, progressions, and transits. In the rare case where there is some serious psychopathology, the astrologer would be better able to assess it and thus to deal with it more intelligently.

In time, as the astrologer's counseling and psychological skills increased, he or she might begin to offer a special kind of astro-therapeutic growth work. With enough additional training, this is all within the range of possibility, since the astrological tools necessitate a profound psychological probing not open to the nonastrological counselor.

The astrologer who sought a counseling and therapy experience of his or her own would have an opportunity for further growth. There are few of us who could not benefit from some kind of psychological growth, and therapy is a major path to that. Furthermore, no learning is as effective as something one has undergone oneself.

Astrologers can further develop professionally, I believe, by reading and discussing with others the great modern psychological authors, such as Jung, Freud, Reich, among others. This can be done either within a university setting or on one's own. The literature of these authors is vast, but even a minimal acquaintance with it is indispensable for anyone in the helping/healing arts.

Finally, astrologers can grow in their skill and vision by gathering together in regular "sharing groups." Much more than conferences, these groups help the astrologer feel less isolated and provide a much-needed outlet for questioning and a source of mutual support and learning. I have been involved with such an ongoing seminar for the past several years. We have been concerned with astrological counseling problems as well as difficulties that pertain to the field of nonastrological counseling and psychotherapy.

The group consists of twelve astrologers and myself, and we meet on a monthly basis for three to five hours. Our general format, not always followed, is this: one of the astrologers will present a counseling problem, for example a case in which a client is particularly stuck and the astrologer has not yet found clarification of the life dilemma nor helped the client sufficiently to more ahead in his or her development.

First, the astrologer presents basic biographical information about the client, how often the client has consulted the astrologer, and the stated concerns and needs of the client. This is followed by a description of the counseling dilemma, the present personality and life situation of the client as far as the astrologer is familiar with these factors, and the recent history of the client relevant to the life problems. This is followed by a description of the upbringing, parents, and family life, as far as that is known. At this point the actual chart and transits are presented.

A general discussion ensues, in which the other astrologers will ask for further information about the case and the astrologer's particular reasons for counseling procedures. Speculations about the counseling problem and valuable insights about the client's life adaptation will be exchanged. Frequently there will be an examination of the astrologer's personal involvement in the counseling situation, including the synastry between astrologer and client. Occasionally, I will bring up concepts and techniques of psychotherapy that are relevant to the case.

Out of the discussion of individual counseling problems, there naturally arises the consideration of general astrological counseling issues. Some of these issues have been the following:

- Problems of excessive dependency on the part of some clients
- Problems of overinvolvement and loss of objectivity on the part of the astrologer
- The recognition of serious emotional problems in the client and the appropriate manner of handling them
- The most effective way of ascertaining the needs of the client
- The need for the astrologer to gain a great deal of information about the client's present state in order to do effective counseling, and with that the need for competent interview techniques
- The need to ascertain the level of life experience and development of the client
- The role and function of counseling in astrology and the question of how to do astro-therapy

We have also used each other as a study group, reading and discussing books from various schools of psychotherapy.

The astrologers and I have grown in several ways from this mutual support and learning, and the group provides, I believe, a good example to other astrologers to overcome their separatism and isolation and to share their difficulties with others who can understand them. To summarize, the astrologers have benefited from the sharing group in the following ways:

- *Support and mutuality.* With the sharing of problems and the understanding of each other's difficulties, they have grown in their sense of professionalism.
- *Development of new insights and options.* The astrologers see more clearly the traps in their counseling, as well as alternative views and new ways of handling difficulties.
- *Greater understanding of the importance of dialogue and exploration.* An appreciation has been gained of the counseling skills of good listening and meaningful questioning.
- *Greater awareness of the importance of knowing the client's level of development and life situation.* In order to do the most effective analysis of horoscope potentials and transit influences, the astrologers have realized how vital it is to gain an understanding of the client's present psychic life and external situation. This has meant that they have had to become even more aware of the need to respect the client's defenses.
- *Greater awareness of the need to keep in touch with what the astrologer is working out in himself.* It has been noted in the group that when an astrologer tends to be involved with a similar type of client or counseling problem over and over again, it represents some unresolved aspect of the astrologer's psyche.
- *Clarification of the various roles of astrologers.* The astrologers have realized that they must examine their unconsidered emotional needs regarding the type of astrological work they do—education, counseling, or therapy.
- *Greater appreciation of the need to learn concepts from psychology and psychotherapy.* One of the aims of the group has been to augment astrology's symbolic depth-psychological knowledge with theory and techniques from modern psychotherapy.

Part II

Counseling and Psychotherapy:
An Introduction for Astrologers

6

Methods of Counseling

Counseling can be defined as a kind of minimal, short-term supportive psychotherapy aimed at assisting an individual to clarify his or her needs and goals in a specific life crisis and establish effective means toward reaching those goals. The counselor helps the client become more aware of her or his true inner needs, feelings, motivations, and goals, while at the same time assessing realistically the social and interpersonal context against which the inner life must be balanced.

It is my contention that astrological counselors can benefit from study of and training in nonastrological counseling as well as psychotherapy. Unfortunately, the nonastrological world of counseling and psychotherapy is not generally cognizant of how much they could be helped by the insights of astrology. However, we are now seeing the first glimmers of change in this regard.

As already stated, astrological counseling has a distinct advantage in its possession of knowledge of archetypal, symbolic processes in nature and the individual. But it lacks specific techniques for helping the individual unburden herself of threatening thoughts and feelings, of exploring with that person her concerns and life, and of appropriately controlling the dynamic relationship between client and counselor.

Although many texts have been written on counseling, and from many different points of view, there are certain procedures that are common to all the diverse theories.

Attitude of the Counselor

The right emotional atmosphere is absolutely fundamental to a good counseling relationship. The most consistently important aspect of counseling is the *attitude* of the counselor, and since it is the initial influence that impresses the client, its impact is magnified. The person needs to feel that he or she is in a safe emotional environment. That means that the counselor will not be shocked or appear judgmental about any aspect of the client's behavior, maintaining an objective, professional attitude, and being personal and real. It is also vital that the counselor have a genuine concern for the client's welfare and growth.

The ability to be a good listener who also asks appropriate and timely questions that show real understanding of the verbal and emotional process of the individual is an important skill in helping the person out of confused and blocked communications and adds to the person's feeling that the situation is safe. (How this differs from therapy is that a competent therapist will allow some silences and blocked communication in order to help the person face and understand his or her fears of silence.)

And finally, the client needs to be helped to perceive the potential for resolution of the problems or crisis that brought her or him to the counselor.

Eliciting the Problem

The following condensed picture of a hypothetical non-astrological counseling case should illustrate for astrologers some of the valuable techniques that can augment their work.

A man in his early thirties consults a counselor because of the fear that he is about to lose a love relationship of several years' duration. Since he feels that he does not have serious, long-term psychological difficulties within himself, he has come to a counselor rather than a therapist to help him through the immediate crisis.

In the first session he portrays for the counselor a picture in which his girlfriend of five years is threatening to break up with him because she feels he is too emotionally reserved, as well as jealous and possessive. The couple had been talking for the last two years of the possibility of marriage—in the good moments. But as the periods of conflict multiply, the girlfriend threatens to end the relationship, even though both have felt that this was the best relationship either of them had ever experienced. Nonetheless, conflicts between them have increased in recent months, and the girlfriend is becoming impatient and angry.

The first phase of counseling consists of the exploration of the problem. This requires not only an ability to establish rapport and emotional contactfulness but also an ability to draw out the client and establish meaning from uncertainty. This depends on the counselor gradually learning to "read" the implications of what the client says and how he says it, which in turn is based on the counselor's possession of a body of knowledge of general human conflicts and needs, character types and defenses, and the dynamics of the counselor-client relationship.

In maintaining a dialogue with this client in ensuing sessions, the counselor will investigate many different facets of the problem. The client will likely be asked under what conditions he becomes possessive and jealous; what his thoughts, feelings, and fantasies are at these moments; and how he generally perceives his girlfriend. The relationship in general will be explored, as well as the client's possible tendencies toward emotional reserve. In the early sessions, the counselor will also be assessing with the client what his goals are for the counseling and the appropriateness of the counseling to accomplish them. With this client, the possibility of referral to psychotherapy was considered by the counselor. Although the client was aware of a need to solve a life problem and the fact that this depended to some extent on an internal change of perhaps a deep nature, the counselor decided he would be able to help the client within the limits of the counseling structure.

As the exploratory phase of the counseling continues, the initial focus of the problem is enlarged to include the relationship in general, the total life picture of the client, and increasingly *the psychology of the client.*

In time, the client came to share details that revealed a greater complexity to the relationship than the initial complaint seemed to indicate. Other problematic areas came to light, as well as the gratifying aspects of the relationship. It was necessary to examine not only the background of the relationship in terms of the total life pattern but also the internal psychology of the client in order for him to gain the support, emotional release, and insights he needed to make a realistic assessment prior to action.

What was discovered was that the male client functioned as the partner who was more stable, supportive, intellectual, and reserved. The woman, by contrast, was more spontaneous, emotional, and outgoing. She apparently needed the man's stability and "rationality" to provide her a stable base for her freer, but still somewhat insecure, personality. He apparently needed her inspirational nature to become more activated and emotional. (There would be astrological correlates to this, of course.) There would probably be a greater emphasis on Earth and fixity in his horoscope, more Fire, cardinality, and mutability in hers. From the Jungian standpoint, we could say that the role of each person represents aspects of the shadow figure of the other.)

Working with Psychodynamics

The term *psychodynamics* refers to the dynamic interaction of diverse forces of the psyche. Typically, the counselor attempts to assist the client to become increasingly conscious of inner conflicts and attitudes and thus to begin to resolve them. In learning to integrate apparently contradictory needs, feelings, and impulses, the client is enabled to feel and act in a more unified way. The counselor accomplishes this by showing the client that he or she is acting one way but feeling another, or feeling two conflicting impulses simultaneously and thus unable to feel deeply committed to either.

The broadest psychodynamic formulations of psychotherapy are those of the conflict of ego, superego, and id, from Freudian theory; persona, ego, shadow figure, and the self, from Jungian theory; and the surface layer, secondary layer, and core, from Reichian theory. In astrological terms, psychodynamics are mirrored in the stressful aspects, an overemphasis on certain elements, signs, or hemispheres; the complete absence of an element; and planets that make operative the polar opposition of houses and signs.

Some of the more specific psychodynamic considerations of modern therapies are the assertion of ego and aggression versus the fear of rejection and abandonment; the assertion of ego and aggression versus moral self-punishment and loss of self-esteem; the need to be strong and independent versus the fear or need to be weak and dependent; the need to be close versus the fear of being engulfed or taken over; the need for intimacy versus the need for autonomy and separateness; the need to be reasonable versus emotional needs. The list is considerably longer, of course.

In the case of our hypothetical reserved and possessive male client, the counselor will keep a mental eye out for the underlying inner motivations and conflicts. Calling upon his general experience of psychodynamics and personality types, the counselor will gradually form an impression of the underlying themes and issues and will *lead* the client's process of thought and feeling toward a clearer demonstration of that impression. It is important, however, that the counselor be flexible enough to see when the first impressions were partially wrong, or even totally incorrect, and then to modify them accordingly. A good technique both for inducing a therapeutic understanding in the client and for keeping the counselor open is that of *reflecting* back to the client in condensed form what he or she is saying but may not be aware of.

As clients become conscious of their formerly unclear inner motivations and needs, and of the meaning of their behavior, the development of insight becomes possible. If the insight is felt deeply as well as understood mentally, the therapeutic effect is that much greater. As we have seen, astrology helps provide those insights from the context of an external source, the horoscope. The value of nonastrological counseling is that it aids the client in gaining his own insight and understanding as a result of the interaction of the client's living expression of his psyche and the counselor's understanding of general human tendencies.

In our hypothetical case, the client and counselor soon realized that the difficulty was as much depth psychological as it was situational, and they agreed to work longer and more intensely than they would have in ordinary counseling. As the pattern of conflict emerged more clearly, the following dynamic picture presented itself: The client perceived his girlfriend as attractive, vivacious, highly sexual, overly emotional in stressful situations, and at times childish and dependent. She appealed to him partly because of her highly energetic, attractive feminine qualities. Furthermore, she was the first person with these traits that he had been able to attract and with whom he could maintain a relationship. In other words, she stirred his more blocked emotional nature, as well as appealing to his male ego by the fact that he could have a relationship with a beautiful woman. Another dynamic feature of their relationship was that her tendencies to more overt insecurity, hysterical fearful reactions, and childlike behavior appealed to a need of his to be a protective, considerate, "strong" male and father figure. He could feel needed and appreciated and she could depend on his stability and rationality.

However, the emotional dynamic that attracted them to each other became, in time, the focus of growing conflict. In order to maintain his self-composed and hyperrational demeanor, he suppressed a good deal of his emotional nature, and his girlfriend felt out of touch with his true self and felt herself too much cast in the role of the overreacting child. He, on the other hand, was fearful that if he really let go emotionally, he would behave in a way that was actually opposite to his usual behavior: He would become a furious, angry man, and his deep vulnerability and pain would be revealed. This seemed like a terrible threat to his self-esteem and provoked the fear that he would surely lose his partner in the process.

With the support and understanding the client received in counseling, he discharged some of his fears and guilt about his inner state and life situation. With growing awareness of what his real conflicts, needs, motivations, and feelings were, he began to see the possibility of a solution to the problem. He realized that he could reveal aspects of his fears and hurts to his girlfriend without having to completely lose his basic sense of himself. This would allow her to be more empathetic toward him and to feel less judged by the strong father image he projected, and it would stimulate her latent capacity to be a strong rational person herself. When some of the pressure of the conflict was thus relieved, the couple could be more at ease. The deeper levels of their problem, originating in their childhood, could then be resolved more gradually, through life experience and/or entering into depth psychotherapy.

Use of Psychological Types

Though not all counselors refer to a specific psychological typology in their understanding of clients, they all use, as part of their diagnostic procedure, impressions of some sort that define the typical ways different kinds of personalities act. Such diagnostic systems of typical psychological behavior provide a useful way of organizing the multifarious and complex manifestations of the human being into a meaningful order. It is similar to the way an astrologer tends to think of a person as a strong Pluto type or a strong Leo type. The astrologer recognizes that the individual's Pluto or Leo emphasis is only a major theme, with many other lesser themes existing side by side. The same holds true of psychological typology; it is not meant to describe the total individual.

While psychodynamics have to do with the conflicts, needs, and motivations within the psyche, psychological typology suggests the typical way these underlying energies are organized and expressed, as well as how they are repressed.

For example, let us take the case of a male client with a strong love-hate relationship with his dominating, somewhat authoritarian father. An underlying psychodynamic of this client might be a conflict between the need to be strong, independent, and authoritative in his actions and the need to be soft, vulnerable, and dependent. Let us say that this particular client has adapted to the conflict by identifying with his father and modeling his behavior after him as he grows up. In the process he must have had to repress access to the soft, vulnerable part of himself, thus cutting himself off from the emotional nourishment he might have received. He has achieved, on the other hand, a degree of success in his life that could only have been attained through aggression, decisiveness, and ego assertion. This typical manner of behavior is his psychological type, or "character structure." The psychological healer will have to consider the client's dominant manner of acting and reacting in the light of the hypothesized underlying motivations. It does not matter if the behavior is given a name, only that it is understood. A Freudian analyst might call this individual a phallic-narcissist. A Jungian analyst might say that the individual is following out a hero-warrior archetype. The astrologer might find an emphasis in Aries, cardinality, and a majority of masculine signs.

Another male might respond to the same exact conflict with the father by identifying with a soft, compliant mother. This man would develop into a somewhat passive adult, for he would have repressed his ability to be assertive. Thus, we would see the same conflict but expressed in an opposite way.

The counselor works with the dominant behavioral mode of the client through her understanding that it simultaneously allows him a sense of ego that gives satisfaction, gives him a vehicle to express himself, and functions as a defense mechanism. The counselor would further need to estimate just how this basic psychological trait would generate interpersonal as well as intrapsychic conflict. In our hypothetical overly assertive and domineering male client, the counselor can explore with him to what degree he is aware of the effect his domineering manner has on himself and others. This dialogue has to be handled with sensitivity and a nonjudgmental attitude, for the client will not be able to look at his behavior if he feels guilty or defensive about it.

In counseling, the aim is to help the client assess the quality and impact of his personality so that he can modify it sufficiently to enable maximum effectiveness in life. In psychotherapy, by contrast, the aim is to alter the character structure of the person in a significant way so that the main traits of the person are no longer functioning defensively. This allows hidden, repressed parts of the total self to become freed so that a more complete and flexible character can develop.

Some of the more typical behavior patterns described in the various psychological typologies are the following: overconfident, aggressive, hard behavior; excessively hyperreactive behavior with provocative and unfocused qualities; rigid behavior with limited spontaneity and feeling; a complaining and suffering attitude; slow, depressed, and self-critical behavior; behavior dominated with extreme fluctuations of mood from depression to elation; clinging, dependent behavior; emotionally detached, shy behavior; confused, distorted behavior. These are some of the more common basic "neurotic" traits. A person usually has one main trait, with one or more other traits or "complexes" that are less dominant, sometimes hidden. Classical psychiatry gives names to the various typical behaviors, calling the person with rigid behavior and limited spontaneity and feeling, for example, a *compulsive individual.*

Counselors need to know the dominant themes in their clients' psyche and behavior. But they also need to be aware that these are only principal qualities, that they vary in intensity depending on the individual, and that other important qualities and attitudes are always involved. We each tend to be a type, but within each of us there lies dormant many types.

The Counseling Relationship

The relationship that develops between counselor and client is contingent not only on the clinical techniques the counselor uses, but also on the unique *gestalt*, or combined whole, of the two interacting personalities. The counseling relationship virtually revolves on this psychological exchange and in particular the attitudes and implicit needs of the client as they are directed toward the counselor. It is the counselor's job to "read" these implicit messages and to respond to them in the most effective way.

Not infrequently a situation of *transference* occurs. This means that the client will sometimes respond to the counselor with needs, attitudes, and expectations that originated in the relationship with the parents and other figures from childhood. While these expectations may have a subjective validity, they are inevitably to some degree inappropriate now. A client who had a very critical and invasive parent, for example, might respond to even simple questioning from the counselor with the feeling that the counselor is being critical. The transference phenomenon will usually be less prevalent in the counseling relationship than it is in therapy because of the shorter duration of the treatment and because the defenses against unconscious childhood feelings and needs are less likely to be opened.

The client's emotional, interpersonal "messages" or transactions are what mainly reflect his or her basic character, or psychological type. Does the client treat the counselor as an absolute authority who has, or should have, all the answers? Does she tend to look for any possible mistakes on the part of the counselor in order to prove him a failure? Or will the client be compulsively pleasant and obliging under all circumstances in an attempt to gain the liking and support of the counselor and avoid possible conflict? Such unconscious defensive maneuvers on the part of the client are not always present in the counseling situation. Frequently the client is an effective co-worker with the counselor. However, clients with well-formed character defenses such as I've illustrated in these three examples, along with many others, do show up, and the counselor should be prepared for them. Although changing the character in a significant way is more typically the task of psychotherapy, a client's character is inevitably an essential ingredient of any immediate life problem, so that it often must be taken into consideration even in counseling.

How should the counselor go about dealing with the client's character structure as it is demonstrated in their interpersonal relationship? Let us take as an example the case of a client who treats the counselor as an unimpeachable authority. The counselor, sensing that the client treats him with excessive respect in order to avoid her own responsibility and authority, can do any or all of the following:

- During the exploration of the problem, the counselor can ask appropriately timed questions to ascertain if the client typically yields initiative and responsibility in life situations. The counselor can then help the client become more aware of this tendency without self-criticism, as well as examine the inner needs and conflicts this behavior expresses and represses. The client can assess more realistically the effect and meaning of this behavior on herself and others. This stimulates the emergence of alternate attitudes.
- The counselor can stimulate the client to bring more of her own opinions and evaluations into the discussion.
- The counselor can explore with the client his fears and concerns about his own authority and knowledge in the counseling situation.
- The counselor can help the client explore her needs and expectations toward him as a "perfect" authority, as well as the client's attitude toward authorities in general.

The psychotherapist will proceed like the counselor but will utilize other procedures as well to deepen the change of the patient regarding the denial of his own authority. Some of these might include (a) encouraging the expression of open criticism or other latent negative thoughts and feelings about the therapist; (b) physically loosening the character and body blocks in order to release emotions, needs, and images, many of which go back to the childhood years, when the attitudes toward authority originated; (c) using fantasy, dreams, imagination, and role playing to free and express unconscious meanings; and (d) generally strengthening all movements toward a positive self-image.

Exploration of the Total Life Situation

Even though the duration of the counseling relationship is usually only a few months and its focus is on a particular phase of the client's life, the more the counselor can visualize the specific problem within the total picture, the more effective the work will be.

In the case of our hypothetical reserved and possessive client, the counselor sought to help him gain insight about causes, meanings, and new ways of action by means of a depth exploration of the problem. In the ensuing dialogue, the counselor utilized his knowledge of general psychodynamics and character structures as well as the information he had of the general nature of the relationship and the interpersonal transactions. Expanding the counselor's knowledge and technique, however, was his ability to elicit the total picture of the client's life pattern. Because of limitations of time and the relative superficiality of the work, however, the counselor has less of an opportunity than the therapist to gain such a valuable impression of the whole.

In the example we are using, the counselor wanted to know what the client's work goals, problems, and sense of achievement were. If his sense of meaningful life direction was being satisfied to some degree, the client would have a solid substructure from which to deal with the relationship crisis. Similarly, if the client did not have other friendships and emotional outlets besides the primary relationship, he would feel especially threatened by its possible loss and would not act with as much freedom of expression as he might otherwise have. Other pressures and concerns outside of the relationship can affect the client, too. Is he concerned about money, a possible illness, guilt and responsibility toward his parents? Is he able to share these outside concerns with his girlfriend? The client might be unconsciously allowing these pressures to interfere with the relationship.

The counselor should also be aware that life-developmental stages are a fundamental part of the total picture. The style and quality of relationship will differ depending on whether the couple is in their middle twenties, late thirties, or early fifties. Individual needs and sensitivities will vary also, depending on whether the partners have never been married before or are each the veterans of a previous marriage. Astrologers are at an advantage in that they bring a particular awareness of the cyclic life changes and their meanings, for example the seven-year Saturnian cycles.

Work on Self-Image

As everyone knows, it always comes back to how one feels about oneself. At moments the world seems like a terrible place, but something happens to change one's state and the world looks different. A cheater suspects everyone else of being a cheater. One begins to feel more worthy, and without one's even trying, people start treating one differently. The individual perception of the self is radiated outward through body expression and the energy field, and others respond to the emanation.

There are many techniques and groups that are predicated on the teaching that you must believe in yourself, that you create your own life, or that there is power in positive thinking. These techniques of moral exhortation are helpful, but they don't confront people with the deeper questions of why and how they feel bad about themselves, so that these knots too often remain buried within the psyche. Unfortunately, any new positive view so attained may not be well grounded. Both the counselor and the therapist need to know how to enter into the dark areas of self-doubt, self-hatred, anger, and rage at others, as well as how to perceive intimations of the person's inner beauty, healthy power, and creativity.

Astrological counseling has an advantage over nonastrological counseling in this respect, too, for the horoscope provides a comprehensive picture of the self-concept and, if utilized in a therapeutic way, can aid the individual in knowing the true, inner person.

The self-concept seems to be a synthesis of several diverse forces: character structure and psychodynamics (which grow out of a combination of basic human instinctual drives and individual responses to childhood experiences), genetics, archetypes, and our unique soul inheritance from past lives.

7

General Psychotherapeutic Procedures

In this chapter I shall examine in more detail some of the basic processes that take place in psychotherapy. It is true that the concerns, principles, and functions astrologers must be aware of in order to work effectively with clients on a continuing basis are generally those of counseling. However, in certain respects the astrological counselor has a much greater connection to depth psychotherapy than does the nonastrological counselor because the horoscope is such an excellent indicator of essential psychological patterns. Thus, the astrologer should be aware of the ways in which psychotherapy proceeds and the kinds of inner processes it deals with, even though he or she may not be immediately involved in the active change of habitual patterns and defenses and the release of potent unconscious forces.

The therapeutic procedures I am about to discuss are complicated, and this shall be the briefest and most introductory of descriptions. It is only an outline and does not describe how an individual therapy process works, only some of the separate aspects of that process. Furthermore, no matter what I could say, it would not meet with universal agreement among therapists.

The Components of Effective Therapy

What makes for effective therapy? We can point to five possible factors: (a) the type of therapy; (b) the competency of the therapist; (c) the sensitivity, maturity, and depth of the therapist; (d) the particular psychological *gestalt* and compatibility between therapist and patient; and (e) the patient's readiness for genuine psychological change.

Type of Therapy

It is significant that people are attracted to different types of therapy. We can speculate that they make their choice according to philosophic and societal values, the particular life-developmental stage they find themselves in, and certain individual considerations as yet not fully known.

This is the kind of question that lends itself to astrology, and some astrologers have attempted to discover the kind of therapy that would be appropriate for a person according to the psychological patterns shown by his or her horoscope. Doris Hebel, in particular, has made some excellent contributions in this regard. For example, a person with a strong Mercury or with an emphasis in the Air signs or the third, seventh, and eleventh houses would do best with a traditional verbal, mental type of therapy. A person with a strong Neptune would do best in a therapy utilizing a great deal of imagination, such as Jungian therapy or psychosynthesis. Someone with an emphasis in Earth or with a Mars-Saturn square would work most effectively in a body therapy, such as bioenergetics or Reichian therapy.

While there is some validity to these correlations, the way in which they are to be interpreted is questionable. The person with an emphasis in Air might feel most comfortable in a highly verbal, mental type of therapy, but she could easily use her well-developed intellectual ability to avoid her emotions. The same can be said for any other highly developed function: It can be used to dominate other areas of the self. Jung has shown that everyone has both a dominant function and an inferior function. While the dominant, most accessible, ability of a person must be utilized to some degree, no matter what type of therapy it is, care must be taken that the ability is not functioning defensively, rather than expressively and developmentally.

Another challenge to the theory that the natal chart can indicate the most effective type of therapy for an individual is the fact that some people make progress with one kind of therapy for a period of time, then come to feel limited by it, and eventually make renewed progress with a different type of therapy altogether. Perhaps this reflects people's tendency to utilize in their first experience with therapy the more accessible parts of their psychological structure as indicated by the major chart emphasis and then later, if continued growth is desired, to make use of the more inaccessible and threatening parts of their personality.

Competency of the Therapist

Although I would certainly agree that the therapist should be well trained and competent, I believe that the importance of other factors is too often minimized. There are some people who believe that all it takes for a therapist to be effective is to learn the techniques of his or her school thoroughly. This notion is predicated on an overly "scientific" view of life, which, in leaving out the human factor, overlooks the essential ingredient in any healing endeavor.

Personality of the Therapist

There have been many studies made of psychotherapy that reveal that it is the kind of person the therapist is and the quality of the relationship between therapist and client that are the major curative factors, whereas the particular therapeutic techniques are only a background and a special language that allow the real healing process to go on. However, as important as the personality of the therapist is, he or she does need valid concepts and techniques in order to deal with the complicated task of working effectively with the mind, emotions, and body of a troubled individual.

The Relationship Between Therapist and Patient

No therapist, no matter how well trained and fully developed as an individual, will succeed in helping every person.

Two other factors will influence the success of the therapeutic process, one of which is the particular personality mix between therapist and client. Since the relationship is one of the key factors in the therapy, the subtle but difficult-to-define ingredients of that relationship are crucial. Therapists with a knowledge of astrology are at an advantage because of their ability to refer to the synastry between the natal horoscopes as well as to the composite chart of the relationship as a whole. It would need the same kind of astrological connections that any good relationship requires: *some* trines and sextiles to facilitate rapport and understanding, *some* hard aspects to energize and challenge; but an overemphasis on either would be counterproductive.

From the nonastrological viewpoint, some of the ingredients are probably related to a sense of mutual respect, similar philosophies of life and societal values, ease of relating, possibility of experiencing conflict from a secure basis, and potential for caring and love. There would also have to be enough character differences so that the patient's latent qualities would be stimulated and supported by the therapist's more developed and accessible traits.

Readiness of the Patient

The final factor in the potential effectiveness of any therapy is the need and readiness of a person for the hard emotional work entailed. Most people will not seek depth therapy unless old patterns and roles are no longer effective, and pain, frustration, and anxiety are becoming intolerable. Other people who are less troubled can do effective work too, but they will be seeking more meaning, satisfaction, and a sense of identity in their lives, which can be a powerful motivating force in itself.

Facets of Psychotherapy

Basic Healing Attitude of the Therapist

It is absolutely necessary that the therapist maintain a supportive, accepting, caring, but objective attitude. This creates the only atmosphere in which patients can share difficult aspects of their personalities for the purpose of eventually integrating them into their total selves. Such an attitude often goes by the name of empathy, but it differs from the caring supportiveness of friendship in that it is consistently more objective and employs specific techniques to help people overcome the blocks that are preventing them from fully experiencing their deeper selves. It is essential that this attitude be genuine and not a mere formality. Patients will inevitably sense whenever the proffered acceptance is not genuine and will feel limited. For the therapy to progress to its farthest levels of growth, it is vital that therapists really care for their patients and even come to think of them as co-workers.

Although it is best that this supportive attitude be fairly consistent, it is also important that the therapist be a human being as well as a capable professional. This means that feelings of annoyance or anger on the part of the therapist can and should be expressed, for they can have a therapeutic value if the relationship between therapist and patient is well established and the patient has some ego strength.

If the therapist finds the empathetic attitude difficult to maintain in a particular therapeutic relationship, however, it may be due to the intrusion of unresolved aspects of his or her own deeper self, and the therapist should have the strength and humility to accept this possibility. Other causes for the difficulty could be an essential incompatibility between therapist and patient or an intractable resistance on the part of the patient.

The demand both from therapeutic training schools and from some patients that the therapist be fully "resolved" or "healthy" interferes with the reality of the situation. As Jung pointed out, in a genuine therapeutic relationship vital aspects of the therapist's personality are being stimulated by the patient, and it is through this stimulation and interchange that the best therapeutic work can be done, so that the therapist grows as well as the patient. Not only astrologers but psychotherapists as well have noted that certain types of people seem to come for help at certain times, corresponding to a particular phase in the professional helper's life in which psychological development and learning are taking place.

Ventilation of Issues

The manner in which the therapist guides and responds to the client's talk is crucial in psychotherapy. But there is a large difference in the extent and type of verbal behavior encouraged in the different schools of therapy.

Generally speaking, ego psychology, the neo-Freudian approaches, existential therapy, transactional analysis, and various of the humanistic psychologies all expect a good deal of verbal exchange, with a significant degree of the therapist's personality being involved and the expression of a certain directiveness. The Freudian approach, on the other hand, attempts to limit the involvement of the analyst to that of a neutral reflector of the patient's projections, facilitator of free association, and interpreter of the underlying motivations and conflicts of the patient through resistances, dreams, slips of the tongue and so on. The strongly cathartic therapies, on the other hand, such as bioenergetics, primal therapy, and Reichian therapy, generally believe that most verbal exchange in therapy is an avoidance of the deeper, repressed emotions and memories. They therefore limit the verbal participation of the therapist, when possible, to the pointing out of the patient's defenses and blocks, the directing of therapeutic procedures, and occasional discussions of the patient's current and earlier life.

The conscious verbal exchange between therapist and patient is nonetheless highly important. It constitutes a good half of the backbone of all psychotherapy. The other part is made up of techniques specific to the different therapies, such as free association, fantasy exploration, acting out of dreams, talking to imaginary parents, exploring subpersonalities, expressing blocked emotions through bodily expression, and so on.

A good verbal rapport between therapist and patient allows the patient to gain support and understanding about difficult life situations and inner emotional states, relieve pent-up feelings, and achieve new insights about his or her behavior and attitudes. The therapist, in turn, learns more about the life struggles of the person, the therapeutic process and needs of the person, and how better to direct that development. It also allows the therapist to confront habitual roles and defenses of the patient whenever she or he is ready to give them up.

In this way, furthermore, the patient has the opportunity to work out his feelings and needs toward authority figures and parental substitutes. Perhaps the patient has a longing for closeness, warmth, understanding, and love. She will have the chance to express this as well as feelings of disappointment, pain, anger, spite, or hatred when the fulfillment of these warm feelings is frustrated due to the reality of the situation. The degree of intensity of the frustration is usually based on the patient's inner conflicts and projections, but it can also be due either to deficiencies in the therapist or to an essential disharmony between therapist and patient.

As effective as therapeutic discussion can be, however, there is just as great a possibility that it can be limiting. Since a person can maintain defenses and control through talk and thereby avoid strong, spontaneous emotion, a repetitious reportage of weekly events can occur, as well as a fruitless intellectual effort to understand causes and meanings. The patient can bring up a series of pains and troubles in order to gain support and confirmation from the therapist without being challenged to see his part in his life difficulties. It is because of this that therapists need techniques to go beyond intellectual-verbal productions.

An example of how a verbal skill can be used defensively is shown by a male patient of mine in his mid-thirties. He talked convincingly about his need to understand and change his "neurotic" patterns, but there was a quality of self-recrimination and forced effort in these intellectual self-examinations, and little or no real depth-psychological change occurred as a result of them. However, after he broke through some of his defenses and allowed more of his emotions to come out, he realized that his previous verbal efforts had helped him to play

out the role of the "good boy" who tries to please the therapist (parents), but that another part of his personality didn't
really want to make those efforts. After this, his fine mental
abilities were used to shed light on, rather than to mask, his real
emotional needs.

Feeling Understood

"Do you know what I mean?" "Do you understand?"
These questions are probably asked more of psychotherapists
than of any others. Generally feeling that they were not sufficiently accepted, loved, or recognized by their parents, patients
need to receive some of the understanding with their therapist
that they never got in their growing-up years.

There seem to be polar aspects to the need to be understood, one general, the other individual. Patients need to feel
themselves a part of the common human life drama, to be like
others, and to know that the therapist understands and can
work with the general problem, conflict, or process they are
undergoing. But as much as there is a need to be like others and
to know that one is participating in universal human and
natural laws, there is an equivalent need to feel different and
unique. This is also implied in the question "Do you understand?" The work of integration is the attempt to achieve one's
individual synthesis of the universal life energy.

A person has a particular and unique life process that the
therapist must gradually come to know in order to be most
effective. The implication here is that the richer and more
varied the life and psyche of the therapist, the more he or she
will be able to "know" and deal with the uniqueness and variations of his or her patients.

Establishment of Trust

In psychotherapy we can distinguish between *initial trust*
and *deep trust*. For therapy to proceed at all, there has to be
sufficient initial trust so that the difficult times can be endured
and the underlying distrust that lies dormant can be brought to
the surface and faced. If initial trust can't be established within

a reasonable period of time, this fact should be recognized and accepted, and the prospective patient should seek out another therapist.

The initial lack of trust may be due to one or more of the following reasons:

- The patient recognizes intuitively that there is an incompatibility between the therapist and himself, in terms of either personality or values and philosophy of life.
- The type of psychotherapy is not appropriate for the person at that particular stage of his development.
- The prospective patient has such severe authority problems that therapy of any kind is inappropriate for him at that time.

Deep, or real, trust has to be established before a person can reach the core of her identity. Such trust grows with the occurrence of the following:

- The patient has experienced a good amount of acceptance, objectivity, support, care, and understanding from the therapist.
- There has been sufficient sharing and discharge of the darker and more threatening parts of the personality, and the patient has seen that the therapist has the emotional strength and therapeutic techniques to deal with them.
- The patient has experienced a degree of real, lasting internal change as a result of the therapy.

Help with Reality Testing

Most people who come for therapy need to learn how to assess more objectively the outer situations of their lives. When the therapist helps the patient in this regard, it is the educational aspect of therapy. Reality testing, or dealing with the objective world, helps a person (a) cope more effectively; (b) see himself reflected in his dealings with others and the effect he makes on them; and (c) become less narcissistic and more mature by realizing that he has to understand and deal with more than his own desires and feelings.

Since there is a certain synchronicity between objective and subjective perception, an improvement in either sphere of functioning will affect the other. If a person becomes more resolved in regard to her own internal conflict and repressed emotion, she will automatically become more unified and in touch with herself on a deeper level. As a result, she will be able to see and deal more realistically with the world.

Heightening of Contact Functions and Awareness

Contact has to do not so much with the "what," or content, of a person's inner and outer life, but rather with the "how," or manner, of his thought, feeling, imagination, sensory awareness, aspiration, action, and body movement.

Genuine contact has three dimensions, and all three are necessary for full awareness. We need to have contact with (a) our inner state, that is, what we really feel and think and what we really need and aspire toward; (b) how we express our inner state to the external world—how we move, our facial expression, tone of voice, quality of speech, and so on; and (c) the needs, feelings, and motivations of those around us. The ability to make contact with all three dimensions is necessary for the development of an integrated self. These contact functions depend on our emotional aliveness, sufficient ego strength, and a readiness to face truths, including painful ones, about ourselves and others.

This aspect of the therapeutic process is the area in which the differences between the various schools of therapy become most evident. Although the following differences are in no way absolute, it could to some extent be said that the Freudian school stresses awareness of that part of one's own mental functioning that is unconsciously based on childhood conflicts; the Jungian school puts one in touch with the imaginative and intuitive processes; while the Reichian and bioenergetic schools emphasize contact with one's somatic and emotional selves.

Utilization of the Therapeutic Relationship

Effective therapy depends not only on the use of well-developed therapeutic skills with a patient who is ready for growth but also on the successful working through of a different and unique exchange—the therapeutic relationship. Like any relationship, it evolves. It consists of an initial phase of liking, hopefulness, and some fear and distrust, followed by deeper contact with certain conflicts and blocks as well as some pleasurable aspects, and eventually a working through of conflicts to the point of genuine sharing and love.

The therapeutic relationship is special and helpful in the following ways:

- The patient is able to live out, in an accepting and objective atmosphere, aspects of her personality that were not able to be expressed with fulfillment in childhood and are too difficult at times with friends and partners.
- Related to the above is the expression and working out of the transference. That is, the patient will tend to project onto the therapist images, feelings, and expectations that actually have more to do with the parents and are not truly appropriate to present-day reality. As these negative or idealized projections and expectations are lived out, voiced, examined, and then gradually resolved with the therapist, it helps the person to mature, let go of inappropriate demands and expectations on those around her, and see herself and others realistically.
- Counterposed to the transference is the perception by the patient of certain qualities in the therapist that the patient will emulate and incorporate into her own ego to some extent. This can help some patients restructure a sense of self that never really developed because of early life deprivations.

Loosening the Defenses

The term *psychological defenses* originated in the Freudian analytic movement, but it is mirrored in the concepts of other schools of therapy: the persona and dominant function, in Jungian analysis; the top dog, in Gestalt work; the character and muscular armor, in Reichian therapy; the strong subpersonality that suppresses other subpersonalities, in psychosynthesis. What this really means is that a certain quality or attitude that is natural to a person becomes exaggerated and overextended in order to hide and help control other aspects of the personality that are felt to be threatening. Security and survival are chosen at the expense of freedom and total expressiveness. For example, under certain circumstances a natural friendliness may become exaggerated until it is a compulsive friendliness which contains within it elements of the natural friendliness but also fear, hostility, and other qualities.

Therefore, defenses are not just artificial adjuncts to the personality that must be demolished before the "real" parts can be released. Defenses are tridimensional: They are repressive, integrative, and expressive. Expressed in our psychological makeup as well as being anchored in our chronic muscular tension, they are partly conscious, partly unconscious.

Effective psychotherapeutic work involves the gradual loosening of the defenses. This means helping the patient release difficult repressed parts of his personality so that they can be lived out in a real way (not merely intellectually) and therefore allow other, more buried parts of his being to be expressed and integrated. Fullness, variety, and liveliness of expression are the result of a decrease in the need for chronic defenses. However, since defenses contain both real and artificial elements, the need to hold on to them for quite a while must be respected by the psychotherapist.

Emotional Release

Although all psychotherapies deal with patients' emotional life, only certain schools seek to evoke strong discharges of emotion directly. Principally these are Gestalt therapy, primal therapy, bioenergetics, core energetics, and Reichian therapy (orgone therapy).

There are four basic categories of emotion that arise: (a)

anger and rage; (b) fear; (c) different forms of emotional pain, such as grief and sadness; and (d) warm emotions, such as love, caring, pleasure, and healthy sexuality. These are not usually unattached experiences but are connected with conflicts, images, needs, and subpersonalities.

Loosening the defenses, if done knowledgeably and systematically, will release various emotions, but it can be a two-edged sword. At its best, it can lead to a rapid sense of change and hopefulness, with greater clarity, liveliness, and expressiveness. But at its worst, it can result in the patient's being stuck by bringing up the same emotion (usually pain or rage) repeatedly without its leading to real change.

One of the reasons for a therapeutic stalemate in emotional catharsis is that there is an incompatible mixture of emotions seeking release: rage, pain, fear, and guilt, for example. Until the fear and guilt are resolved, the rage and pain cannot find a genuine release. Furthermore, one emotion can be used as a defense against another emotion—for example, anger as a defense against pain and crying, or vice versa. Also, a patient may find it possible to express one kind of emotion in the presence of the therapist but not another, due to unresolved transferential feelings.

There are many theories of the origin of anxiety. It is said to result from (a) a blockage of libido; (b) more stimuli than the nervous system and psyche can integrate; (c) any experience that is a signal to the ego of a serious threat to its ability to maintain a sense of security and self-image; (d) any major experience of the unknown. In any truly therapeutic process, a person will have to experience some anxiety, since the alteration of any chronic attitude, habit, or defense will feel like a threat. But an excessive and prolonged degree of anxiety interferes with therapeutic progress. Intolerable anxiety is a basic driving force in the formation of defenses and neurotic symptoms.

Rollo May has pointed out that our emotions have two, inseparable aspects. They are reflective of the past, "caused by" experiences from the past, and to understand them we look at the "reason why" they exist. Emotions push us from behind, as it were. But equally, they are progressive, for they represent the way we want ourselves and our lives to become. Thus, they are a pull from ahead and are involved in creative aspiring. There is a "purpose for" our feelings and emotions, and this involves intentionality and life aims.

Integration

Only with the breakdown of defenses, the consequent release of repressed emotions and needs, and the development of genuine insight can integration of unconscious elements into the personality occur. And even with all of these prerequisites fulfilled, integration requires time, repetition, and habituation. It also necessitates quieter periods in therapy after emotionally intense ones.

Growth of Insight

I would make a distinction between *intellectual insight* and *genuine insight*. Although insufficient in itself, intellectual insight can aid a person to begin the process of work on the self but is easily used in a negative way, as a buttress against feeling and spontaneity. Genuine insight, on the other hand, comes into being when one begins to open up one's defenses, lives through a difficult life experience in an emotional way, or attempts to understand a situation in one's life through the taking of full responsibility for oneself. Lack of genuine insight is one reason why a person tends to remain stuck in an ineffective emotional pattern. Such a situation is fairly well indicative that the person is not really seeing into and accepting his active role in maintaining the conflict.

Many people think of insight as having to do only with a fresh understanding of causation from the *past*. But it can also function *dynamically*, as a new way of looking at the present-day interplay of forces and needs, and *purposively*, as a stimulating recognition of the meaning of one's activities in terms of future goals.

Release of Guilt and Shame

Almost everyone has a hidden, secret part of his or her psyche. Until this hidden secret is shared by an accepting therapist, there will always be a limit to the progress one can make in therapy. This, then, is the confessional aspect of psychotherapy.

The content of that part of the personality for which we feel shame varies considerably: It may include inadequate or unusual sexual experiences or fantasies, impulses of meanness or sadism, generalized feelings of inadequacy, feelings of being infantile, a particular event in the past about which one feels guilty, identification with a hated parental trait, and so forth. The sharing of previously hidden guilty or shameful aspects of oneself has a potent effect on the growth of one's self-esteem and differs significantly from the semiconscious use of guilty or inadequate feelings. Easily shared and habitually used to keep from feeling stronger and more assertive, the latter is in fact a defense.

Evolution Toward a Healthy Self-image

If there is one aspect of personal growth that is universally worked with in the various schools of therapy, it is the patient's discovery of an authentic self-image. Yet this can only be found by excavating through the overlay of the many conditioned roles, masks, and exaggerated behaviors. The main thesis of most psychotherapies is that the way a person really sees himself will condition the way the world sees and treats him. In this way the person gets confirmation of some deep belief about existence, which is in fact only a reflection of his self-image. As the saying goes, character is destiny. By providing a safe emotional atmosphere, interpretive understanding of underlying processes, and specific techniques for opening up the unconscious, the therapist hopes to stimulate a natural healing process of deep self-recognition.

The particular image a person has of herself at any moment depends on the level of the psyche she is operating from. If the only self-image a person can tolerate comes from the surface of the psyche (or persona), it will have a degree of protectiveness or defensiveness about it. But if it reflects the next deepest level of the psyche, the level of repressed needs and emotions, the self-image will take on a color of aggression, vulnerability, fear, dependency, and so on. Deeper still is that part of the psyche in which the true self resides—the core. When the self-image is based on that, qualities of genuine self-confidence and love shine through. (A fuller discussion of the three levels of the psyche can be found in the conclusion of this book.)

People have more than just one underlying self-image. Astrologically, the various themes can be seen to correspond to the major configurations, strong planets, and other factors in the natal horoscope. Psychologically, the underlying self-images are related to psychodynamic conflicts but are not identical with them. For example, one underlying conflict may be the subjective experience of abandonment by the parents, and the buried child within the person feels he was treated extremely unfairly as a result. Out of such a conflict one person might develop the attitude or self-image of an angry, bitter child, whereas another person might see herself as a poor, innocent waif. Many different attitudes, complexes, or self-image formations can develop from the same conflicts. And a person can have several different self-concepts operating at different levels of the unconscious simultaneously; for example, the waif image can be used to cover up a deeper, less acceptable attitude of bitterness.

Strengthening the Will

The role of the will is not talked about very much in modern psychotherapy, since it is associated with the nineteenth-century Victorian moralistic notion of "will power." However, exceptions to this occur in the theory of psychosynthesis, core energetics, and in the writings of Rollo May.

It is my belief that all sound psychotherapy activates a function in human beings best described as the will. Different from will power, which overemphasizes purpose, discipline, and morality at the expense of desire and feeling, the will takes into account both the immediate wishes of a person and the long-term goals. Psychotherapy invariably attempts to support and stimulate the client to take action appropriate to both the hard struggle to achieve and the more immediate needs for pleasure and gratification.

The Use of Dreams, Fantasy, Imagination

In this function of psychotherapy we can see the greatest variations in therapeutic approach. For most people, patients and therapists alike, it is usually the most pleasurable part of the therapy, as well as the most creative and individual. The Freudian and Jungian analytic methods, psychosynthesis, and Gestalt therapy have done the most extensive work with it.

The ability to tap this aspect of the psyche, has several therapeutic advantages:

- It combines aspects of the mental, emotional, and intuitive functions of a person in a unitary synthesis. The mental component of a person is utilized, but intellectualization is usually avoided.
- Since a person's dreams, images, and fantasies seem to be more uniquely her own than perhaps anything else, a sense of creativity, individuality, and accomplishment is achieved.
- It provides an almost direct link with the unconscious, more so than any other activity, with the exception of spontaneous body movement and expression.

But like any other powerful tool, this path of exploration can be overused. For when this aspect of a person is activated to the point where it dominates all others, the result is an almost exclusive attention to the inner world to the neglect of one's interaction with others.

The Reliving of Childhood and
Resolution of the Relationship with the Parents

This is the most complex and difficult of therapy functions to describe. A few psychotherapies have little to say about it, but any theory that accepts the existence of unconscious factors in the human psyche will have to deal with it. One of the difficulties in achieving a unified approach in the helping/healing arts is the tendency of people to think in either/or terms. Either we deal largely with present living and inner life, or we deal with the past. Humanistic psychology was born out of a legitimate need to balance the psychoanalytic tendency to pay too much attention to childhood and to virtually blame the parents and the early life for a person's present difficulties. But however necessary was the impulse to correct this imbalance, there is sometimes a tendency in therapy now to pay too much attention to present life. This, too, limits its effectiveness and fails to help people reach their core or self. Any organic approach, which provides for the discovery and expression of all functions of the human being in the present, will ultimately lead to images, memories, feelings, and needs related to the past as well as the present. The human being is a process of unfolding and not a static entity.

Simplifying the picture somewhat, we could say that patients arrive at the important stage of reliving childhood and resolving their relationship with their parents according to the following sequence of steps:

1. The gradual loosening of the depth defenses. This should be attempted in therapy only after rapport has been established with the therapist and the patient has developed some ego strength, as well as acquired some sources of security and satisfaction in his or her work life, friendships, and personal life. Unfortunately, some therapists will confront strongly based defenses before these conditions are established.

2. The breakdown of the defenses will lead to the release of repressed emotions, attitudes, needs, memories, and subpersonalities. Since the defenses are partially comprised of feared aspects of the parents that have been incorporated, the breaking down of these defenses results in our becoming less like our parents. The newly released emotions, attitudes, "selves," are those parts of our child nature that could not be lived out in childhood but are more truly our own.

3. With the release of the repressed child, the patient can go on to satisfy some unmet developmental needs as well as other aspects or subpersonalities of the total self that are appropriate to the current life. Thus, the patient gradually lets go of hatred and rage toward the parents, as well as the frustrated longing for love from parental substitutes, and becomes truly adult.

Exceptions to this pattern are those patients who come for psychotherapy already explicitly childlike. These kinds of people use their childlike behavior as a defense against living fully in the world in an active, responsible way. Examples of this behavior are an excessive innocence and naïveté, a clinging dependency, an unwillingness to handle money obligations, a hysterical emotionalism, or a prolonged social withdrawal. In this kind of situation, the patient will have to build up more ego strength and adult defenses before undergoing the process of breaking down prior defenses and reliving childhood.

Development of a Life Purpose

This function of the psychic life is seldom written about in psychotherapeutic texts (with the exception of the trans-personal psychologies), but it is nevertheless a significant aspect of therapeutic work, both as a long-term goal and as a part of the immediate ongoing process. Somewhere along the line, every patient asks, "Where am I going with my life?"

Although no definition of so loose a term as *life purpose* will ever achieve universal agreement, the following can be said: A sense of life purpose involves goals that motivate and energize a person to move, to grow, to want to live. It has special meaning for a person that is lasting in time, that gives a sense of accomplishment beyond practical security and the satisfaction of biological needs, although these are included within it. Many a person has come to a therapist in his thirties or forties reporting that he has achieved success in all the goals he has set for himself (career, home, family, and so forth), yet still he feels a sense of dissatisfaction and purposelessness.

A life purpose has two faces and each reflects the other:

- The personal goal is that of *true self-knowledge and self-mastery.* Until a person truly knows herself in all her depth and variety, and has synthesized some unity from it, there will be a sense of dissatisfaction.
- The other, more social aspect is the deep need, often unconscious, to feel oneself a part of the great cosmic stream of life, to *participate with and contribute to others.*

Part III

Common Astrological
Counseling Problems:
A Psychotherapist's View

NOTE: In the following section, I shall consider some of the more typical problems astrological counselors come up against. I have not tried to be exhaustive, but have defined several broad areas that are familiar to me from the astrological sharing group of which I am a part and from astrologers' books and lectures. Since I am not an astrologer, I have focused upon these hypothetical situations with a *psychotherapist's* understanding, with the aim of highlighting and clarifying some of the deeper issues and meanings in a general sense. The more fully aware astrologers become of the true significance of their clients' behavior, the more likely they will be to find specific techniques of their own in each individual counseling situation.

8

The Troubled Love Relationship

Of the various types of clients who tend to go to astrologers, one of the most frequently seen is the client who is in a prolonged difficult love relationship and can't seem to change it or who has a pattern of unsatisfying relationships.

Here, for instance, is one astrologer's report of such a situation:

> A woman came to me saying, "My life is lousy, and I want to do something more with it." As we worked through her chart, she told me that her main problem was a young man with whom she was professionally and romantically involved. Since he had come into her life, her business had begun to suffer, her children had started giving her problems, and she herself had become physically ill. As she spoke, she decided that the right course of action would be to end the relationship, but she wanted to know from me if that would solve her problems. I could only tell her that it was up to her, that she was responsible for the quality of her life and that no one could predict the future. She left stating that she was going to disengage herself from this man.
>
> However, the next time I saw her, she told me she had decided that ending the relationship was not the answer, and she wanted to know what else she could do to improve her life. Again we talked about alternatives and focused on dealing with the immediate problems. She again decided on a course of action and asked for my reassurance that all would go well—which again she did not get. I did ask this time, however, "If you are so unhappy, could any action make it worse?" Her answer was that at least she knew what she had, so why should she go through all the hassle of changing things if I couldn't guarantee that her life would be better?

Here we see a dependent type of individual who is stuck in a very limiting and painful relationship. Her dependency is shown by the fact that she wants to be told exactly what to do by the astrologer. What we cannot do as helpers in the healing arts is to jump to some oversimplified answer about this kind of person. In other words, we cannot simply explain away our failure to help such people make changes in their lives by saying that they are self-destructive or masochistic and that that's all there is to it. The person in a difficult relationship is making an implicit emotional statement via the relationship. Such statements have two general directions, one having to do with the self, the world, and the present, and the other referring more to the past and the parents.

Statements about Oneself and the Present

One of the major tenets in the psychology of relationships, recognized by both astrologers and psychotherapists, is that difficult aspects of the partner usually represent the repressed part of oneself. This is because in order for a person to accept and release a repressed and threatening part of herself, there must be an external stimulus of a similar kind. For example, if a person has repressed her sense of personal power, her positive anger and her force (described astrologically as her Mars energies), she will never be challenged to express that part of herself if her environment is always peaceful and nonconflictual. However, a challenging partner will force her to deal with it. The implication here is that if this kind of person feels blocked in her relationship, it is probably because she is not responding to the challenge appropriately and effectively.

Sheldon Kopp, in his book *If You Meet the Buddha on the Road, Kill Him*, wrote in this regard:

> To some extent, each of us marries to make up for his own deficiencies. As a child, no one can stand alone against his family and the community, and in all but the most extreme instances, he is in no position to leave and to set up a life elsewhere. In order to survive as children, we have all had to exaggerate those

aspects of ourselves that pleased those on whom we depended, and to disown those attitudes and behaviors that were unacceptable to them. As a result, to varying degrees, we have each grown into disproportionate configurations of what we could be as human beings. What we lack, we seek out and then struggle against in those whom we select as mates.[6]

Another possibility is that the unfulfilling relationship is a statement of a poor sense of personal worth. The masochistic self-putdown satisfies several neurotic needs: (a) It limits one's assertiveness and therefore keeps one from being severely criticized, rejected, or abandoned. (b) It keeps one attached to the parents and the past inasmuch as that is the locus where the poor self-concept began. (c) It is an indirect accusation of the partner, implying that he or she is the cause of the suffering. The masochistic complaint, whether tacit or explicit, that says, "You see how much you make me suffer?" is in fact a form of indirect anger, at times even sadism. (d) It protects one from the struggle and responsibility of doing something with one's life.

A common pattern that I have seen in therapy patients who are stuck in a chronically difficult relationship is the following: The person doesn't feel ready for a mature and sharing relationship but, denying this inner state, finds herself in a compromise relationship. Secretly knowing it won't work, she struggles to make it so with effort, fantasy, and illusion. Disappointment and conflict with the partner, along with blame and accusation, ensue. Somewhere within herself the person knows that she made the wrong choice from the beginning.

Oftentimes the painful relationship challenges the person to confront a defensive role. For example, a man may have a tendency in relationships to take the role of the stronger, more understanding person, acting somewhat like a protective parent, but as a result denying many of his own needs and feelings. He feels denied, because he doesn't ask or his role doesn't permit

---

[6] Sheldon Kopp, *If You Meet the Buddha on the Road, Kill Him* (New York: Bantam Books, 1976), p. 70.

it. At some point this man may find himself becoming gradually more aware of the role he has assumed, with all of its limitations and its self-destructive aspects. If he doesn't feel compelled to terminate the relationship as a result of this new awareness, he may begin to modify his habitual posture or even to let it go.

A painful and difficult relationship can stimulate an emotionally blocked person to feel more. And, if it does not remain unchanging, such a relationship can give a person with a poor self-image an opportunity to make contact with her or his emotional needs, typical roles and defenses, and the way in which other people see one. It has been said that we can see ourselves only as we are mirrored in our relationships.

Finally, remaining stuck in a negative relationship can be a statement of belief that without it one would be even worse off. The person feels that being alone will be even more difficult than the present painful situation, that there is "no one out there for me," and that he is not prepared to face the struggle of beginning again. When people are overly concerned about the deficiencies they may find in others, they are frequently saying that they themselves feel inadequate.

Statements about One's Parents and the Past

When the partner represents the parent of the opposite sex, which is frequently the case, the picture is much more complex than one would think at first glance. First of all, the person is trying to get the parent to change, symbolically, through the partner. Until we become more thoroughly integrated, there is always a tendency to project onto love partners expectations and images that were first experienced toward the parent. We want our partners to become more loving, accepting, approachable, affectionate, reasonable, emotional, whatever, according to the perceived deficiency of the parent. The partner never makes it, of course, and the person is forever trying to get him or her to change. If the partner were to change, the hidden wish says, then one's unfilled childhood needs and feelings could be realized and one would feel complete.

There is another side to this, however. On the one hand, one hopes to get one's partner to fulfill the image one has of the "good parent." But there is an opposite need as well—to express one's feelings fully to the "bad parent," who is symbolized by this same partner. There is always the unconscious longing to express one's deepest hurt, pain, anger, and rage in ways that were not allowed in childhood. This complex dynamic is what accounts for some of the intensity of conflict one sees in relationships where the actual situation doesn't seem to warrant it.

One of the most common conflicts I have observed in the relationships of my therapy patients in this regard is the following: One of the partners feels that the other is neglecting the expression of care, sensitivity, or emotionality. The other person feels that the partner is exaggerating or making excessive demands and withdraws even further. This turns into the battle of "the demander" versus "the withholder." Both are convinced of the correctness of their position, and the assertions of each only reinforce the fears and conflicts of the other. Although both feel securely "rational" in their position, the emotional fact is that "the demander" is usually overreacting based on some childhood wound or unmet need, while "the withholder" is unconsciously provoking the partner because of fears of intimacy and being controlled and could express more feeling and need in the situation.

Another possibility is that the partner represents the parent of the same sex. For example, a woman might be looking to fulfill, via the sexual experience with her male partner, a need for soft, nurturing contact that was missing in her relationship with her mother. But if the man who is her partner is incapable of tenderness, or if she herself is unable to distinguish between her need for passionate sexuality and her need for affectionate tenderness, she will never really be fulfilled.

Finally, it is common to see people behaving in a counterproductive fashion simply because they are playing out the role of the parent of the same sex—for example, the man who is passive and submissive to a dominating woman because his father acted that way with his mother.

Although I have broken down these factors into categories for the purpose of simplification, some or most of them will operate in various ways in every troubled relationship. Nor should it be forgotten that even in the most difficult relationship, there are some pleasurable aspects, so that every such involvement will be a combination of the difficulties just described along with some more fulfilling aspects. The counselor also has to be aware of the possibility that a client will sometimes exaggerate the negative aspects of a relationship or fail to talk about the more positive ones. This can be so for two reasons: in order to complain about the partner rather than face him or her directly and to avoid responsibility for some part of the difficulties.

Schematically, we can distinguish between three types of love relationship: (a) destructive; (b) developmental; and (c) fulfilling. There are, of course, many gradations between them. In the *destructive relationship* there is a preponderance of hurt, suffering, and impediments, with no emotional growth and learning and with a diminishing sense of self. In the *developmental relationship*, there can be much struggle and conflict, but the partners grow in understanding, feeling, and self-awareness. In a *fulfilling relationship* there is a preponderance of sharing, growth, and love, and this kind of relationship is achieved usually after a person has experienced much life experience and one or more developmental relationships.

9

The Dependent Client

One of the foremost counseling problems described by astrologers is the excessive dependency of some of their clients. (This is particularly true of those who see clients repeatedly, especially on demand.)

One astrologer wrote me this communication:

> The greatest problem I have in astrological counseling is the client's dependency on me. For example, one woman called to ask if she should look for a job that day. I said yes, if she needed one. I told her that she could look for a job on a so-called bad day and get the job on a "good" day. Besides, do we really know what a "good" day is? Squares can be very energizing, and so forth.
>
> Another serious problem, and it is obviously related to the first, is the need to deal with the client's desire for absolute predictions. I don't believe astrologers are infallible, and when they think they are, their ability to counsel is lessened. Yet, convincing clients that self-knowledge, and not knowledge of the future, is what they need, is one of the astrologer's greatest challenges.
>
> Finally, and this is a personal problem of mine, I feel the need to keep on giving as long as the client is asking. One of my first readings continued for five hours until I practically lost my voice. I now limit my readings to two or three hours.

My correspondent is correct in her intuition that the development of dependency is not the client's problem alone but is an outgrowth of an improperly handled astrologer-client relationship. Anyone who wants to avoid this problem should be on the lookout for the following predisposing factors:

- Excessive use of predictions without examining the psychological issues
- Excessive one-directional advice giving
- A client with a shaky ego who is afraid of psychotherapy
- A client who expects magic from the astrological information
- The astrologer's unsatisfied parenting needs
- The astrologer's difficulty saying no to the hurt and needy part of himself that he sees in the client
- The astrologer's need to be an oracle or particularly impressive

All of this notwithstanding, the client herself may have a pattern of dependency, which is actually composed of diverse qualities and implicit psychological statements. It is important for the counselor to understand these psychodynamic patterns, inasmuch as exploring the deeper meaning and function of the client's behavior can sometimes help to modify it. However, in this (and in every) case, it is essential for the counselor to be sensitive to the client's readiness to assess the habitual and defensive behavior. In the pages that follow I shall explore the inner meaning of dependency.

Independence means being adult, responsible, and active in the world. Yet some people have not yet developed a sufficient sense of self to do that effectively. Astrology, and the astrologer, can function positively as a haven, a source of support, and a means of growth for the person who needs gradually to build up this sense of self before becoming more independent; here is where astrology can be therapeutic. The astrologer can know that it is this simple type of dependency when the client is growing and gradually dropping dependency demands.

In a second, highly prevalent kind of dependency, however, there is the implicit message from the client to the astrologer, and to the world, that he or she is helpless and needs to be taken care of. It is an appeal for an all-nurturing parent. This pattern differs from the first only in the degree of the sense of helplessness deriving from an absence of real nurturance from the parents in childhood. There may also be some inherent lack of sense of drive that is difficult to change.

One dependent patient of mine expressed this aspect of her personality in the therapeutic sessions by demonstrating marked difficulties in initiating anything. She demanded that I take the lead on every issue or technique. "You have all the answers, why don't you tell me what to do?" she would sometimes say. Eventually we found that her inhibition about more active participation in the therapy process was based on a fear of making mistakes. (She had a "correct," judgmental mother) as well as an indirect demand that I take care of her and nurture her as her mother had not. Furthermore, her passivity and dependency was a way of inhibiting an inner sense of power she felt she possessed but could misuse. (She had the Sun, Jupiter, and Pluto in Leo in the first house.)

Can the astrological counselor consciously do some minimal "re-parenting" for this kind of client to help fulfill the deep childhood need and thereby release the person from the childlike dependency? Or will it just reinforce the dependency strivings without resolution and growth to maturity? The same question beleaguers the psychotherapist also, of course, and is all the more troubling since there is an especial likelihood of prolonged dependency in psychotherapy. The answer is a qualified yes: Some *minimal* reparenting can be effective with *some* individuals, but not so with others. To a certain degree this is based on trial and error and therefore should be done cautiously.

A third motivating factor that unconsciously influences a person is that becoming more independent means joining the world of adults, yet the individual may see that world as essentially aggressive, egotistic, and insensitive. This kind of person is afraid of contacting his own aggressiveness and power drives for fear of misusing them as they were misused against him. He is determined not to be like the aggressive, insensitive parent he feels he had. However, it is interesting to note that on an unconscious level this person will have identified with the cruel parent to some degree. This is impossible to see directly, but it can perhaps be deduced if the person comes across as overly gentle and submissive.

Another aspect of this is that remaining dependent and demanding excessive attention represent an indirect, camouflaged attack on the parent as symbolized by the therapist or astrologer. This kind of person, full of unrecognized spite and anger, is fervently holding on to authority figures on the one hand and denying them any real authority or power on the other.

Finally, some children have been taught to be dependent because any expression of independence and assertiveness was a threat to the parent's sense of authority. In such a case, being independent means being punished and abandoned.

The several themes I have just described that typically underlie dependent behavior are not the total explanation, simply the innermost meaning of the dependency statement to the self and to the world. Astrologers are familiar with the principle that particular aspects or configurations cannot be dealt with in isolation but must be understood in terms of the total chart. The same holds true for dependency. For example, if the main theme of a client's dependency is the need to be taken care of by a loving parent, then further exploration of this question will reveal other aspects of the client's needs and attitudes. There would undoubtedly be problems of assertion, fears of abandonment, and a poor self-image. Depression, too, can easily be a concomitant, since both tendencies, if they are marked, originate in the early nurturing period of life. Thus, the significance of the dependency would be amplified and would have to be seen as part of a *gestalt* along with other major aspects of the personality.

The other side of the coin to the dependency strivings of the client is the presence in the astrologer of conflict about parenting and nurturing. Undoubtedly, some people who are in the position of provider and authority in the healing arts have at least some minimal problems in this regard. The counselor and healer, if conscious and motivated, can work on her or his own side of the conflict to improve or resolve it. However, the astrologer who encounters frequent problems of dependency in clients should suspect the persistence of a significant amount of unresolved conflict in himself.

Psychological difficulties are usually the result of several factors, not just one "cause." Nevertheless, one aspect can be deeper and more basic than the others. The following is a description of several of the factors possible in the unresolved need of the astrologer caught in a dependency situation in counseling.

Identification with the Parents

Since astrology, like any healing art, is functionally similar to the parenting function, providing as it does support, advice, guidance, and wisdom, the stimulation of parental issues is great for the astrologer. And like any healer, the astrologer can easily identify unconsciously with the dominant parent in her life, especially if there is a significant degree of inner conflict and defenses. (The other parent is identified with on a different level.) But if the astrologer doesn't have any training in counseling, with all the theoretical structures and practical procedures that it provides, then she will inevitably fall back on the parental role as her model of behavior in the authority position. If the particular parent in question was highly directive or judgmental, the astrologer would tend to act like that parent at moments of stress or uncertainty, as much as she might consciously reject such behavior. And these tendencies would, of course, reinforce a dependent type of client.

At the same time, it is natural to suppose that the astrologer would be making every effort to be different from her parents, trying not to make the same mistakes and struggling toward individuality. Thus, the astrologer who herself had a critical and judgmental parent will probably be sure to be especially supportive and nonjudgmental, and this will reflect genuine qualities of her deep self. Nevertheless, another part of her psyche will have introjected that parent and so contain elements of him or her. One of the tasks of the professional helper is to become aware of the internalization of models of behavior from parents and teachers and to sift out what is no longer useful, retaining the productive aspects of that learning experience.

Identification with the Child in the Client

An astrologer may become overly involved with a particular client because he unconsciously sees the hurt, lost, confused, fearful, or angry "child" part of his own psyche. Furthermore, if that psychic component is particularly threatening, and therefore largely repressed, then the astrologer might be tempted to protect at all costs, or resolve at great speed, the similar but more obvious quality in the client. The astrologer would thus reinforce any dependent inclination on the part of the client. If the astrologer finds a dependent relationship developing, she should look for possible overprotectiveness on her part. By honestly examining what it is in the client that is being protected, the astrologer can learn more about her own unfulfilled child nature.

Feeling Inadequate about One's Competency

Any professional helper in the healing arts is prone to feeling dissatisfied with his performance occasionally. This is particularly true of beginners in the field. Astrologers often compensate for their feelings of guilt or inadequacy by giving too much time, overprotecting clients, or being fearful of setting limits. Astrologers have the added responsibility of knowing that astrology is not accorded serious recognition in our society. Also, the client may have unfounded expectations of the consultation and/or be in different emotional straits. It is in this area particularly that astrologers can help themselves by forming close peer groups for support, the sharing of mutual problems, and the improvement of counseling skills.

Unfulfilled Needs to Be a Therapist

As I have stated earlier, some astrologers are particularly interested in allowing their work with clients to take on a therapeutic function. They see clients frequently and regularly and attempt to facilitate an ongoing deep psychological change. This kind of situation can be helpful for the client if the astrologer is sensitive to the client's readiness for change and has good skills in the handling of relationship dynamics and the interpretation of conflict, but such a situation is ripe for dependency.

Strong Synastry with the Client

One of the powerful lessons that has come out of the astrology sharing group in which I participate is the observation that the astrologer can be caught in a kind of bind with a client when the natal potential of the client is especially challenging to that of the astrologer. What happens is that the astrologer is stimulated, whether consciously or unconsciously, to understand the client better in order to understand himself better. (Carl Jung, in *Modern Man in Search of a Soul*, contended that in curing a patient, the psychoanalyst cures himself.) This means that the astrologer is likely to become too personally involved with the case, giving more of his time and energy, with a possible consequent outcome of dependency on the part of the client.

A strong synastry between astrologer and client does not necessarily mean that a dependency will develop, however, only that the astrologer will feel some special affinity with the client or the potential for a special openness. But the affinity can be either positive or negative. In the case of positive affinity, the astrologer might have in common with the client certain soft aspects or other astrological configurations that he or she feels particularly comfortable with or approving of in his own chart. For example, an astrologer might feel very good about his Sun-conjunct-Venus in Leo. He might therefore be particularly open to a person with a similar configuration, even if it was not conjunct his planets. In the case of a negative affinity, however, the sharing might have to do with certain aspects, planets in certain signs, or certain house emphases that have troubled the astrologer. The astrologer could therefore be magnetized by conflicts in the client that are similar to his own and will work especially hard with this person.

Finally, there is the possibility of a counseling challenge when the particular quality in the astrologer's chart that is the most difficult, submerged, and threatening happens to correspond to an accessible, freer quality in the chart of the client. For example, an astrologer might have Mars in the twelfth house squaring Pluto in the third house, while the client might have Mars in the first house trine to Pluto in the fifth house. This latter combination of energies would possibly be more accessible to consciousness and action for the client.

In any of the situations just discussed there is the potential for a bind occurring in the counseling relationship. In these cases, both the client and the astrologer suffer.

10

The Depressed Client

Periods of depression, anxiety, and uncertainty commonly serve as the motivating stimulus that brings people to consult an astrologer or a psychotherapist. But the client with a depressive quality that has become a chronic part of the person's life, not just as a transitory and exceptional phase but as a minor key or a major motif, presents an astrological counseling problem and is the subject we shall deal with in this chapter.

Depression that has taken on the function of a quality of the personality is actually part of a larger picture of poor self-image and difficulty asserting one's needs and deeper feelings. Impaired work functions and social and personal relations are also invariably involved. On a physical level, there is a generalized energy block and contraction. Some people will attempt to conceal the depression—with either an air of bravado, an excessive striving in their activity, or a diminished emotional responsiveness. (The behavioral change that is part of the more extreme swings of mood known as manic depression is due to somewhat different unconscious conflicts and developmental need frustrations.)

It is important to differentiate between a *depressive trait* and a *depressive character.** When a person has a tendency to

---

*This important differentiation of character trait and character structure was made by Elsworth Baker, M.D., in his book *Man in the Trap* (published by the Macmillan Company, New York, 1967).

depression among several other attributes but it does not dominate her or his emotional response, it is a trait. If depression is
the major mode of response to conflict or stress, the person has
a depressive character. In the latter case the depressive attitude
pervades the total being of the person and altering it presents a
more challenging therapeutic task.

Although many types of conflict and disturbance can lead
to depression, the predisposition to having a depressive character can be traced to the first year of life, when emotionally
nourishing contact between mother and infant, particularly
nursing, may have been limited.* Modern psychology also explains depression in the following ways:

- When anger is not expressed outwardly and immediately
  to the appropriate person, it has to go somewhere, so it
  gets retroflected back upon the self as self-criticism and
  a stasis of emotional energy. This results in depression.
- Freud said that one component of depression can be the
  symbolic and unconscious grieving for a lost loved person. Here, too, there may be a connection with repressed
  anger, inasmuch as one may unconsciously anticipate the
  loss of a loved person if one dares express anger toward
  that person. But unexpressed anger will always seek discharge and will come out in fantasy, dreams, or other
  indirect ways. Therefore, in a subjective sense, the person is already experiencing the loss of love, and with that
  a primary motivating force in life.
- A third explanation coming from Freudian theory is that
  depression can be attributed to a "harsh superego"; that
  is, the person is inwardly critical of herself for not reaching some high standard of behavior (the ego ideal), or
  conversely, does something considered punishable or
  "bad." Both introjections of the values and standards of

---

*This theory of the predisposition to depression is not held by all
modern psychologies. The schools of psychology and therapy that share
this belief are the Freudian, neo-Freudian, object-relations theory, Reichian, and bioenergetic schools.

parents and society, according to standard psychoanalytic theory. (In my therapeutic practice, I have found that patients' ego ideals seem to be admixtures of identifications with parental and societal values and a natural and individual potential for achievement that a person feels intuitively and strives to attain. From this point of view, the ego ideal is not just some artificial construct to be rejected totally.)

- Any vital need or feeling that is blocked or unexpressed long enough can lead to depression or anxiety. This theory originates from psychosomatic therapies, such as the Reichian approach, and also from various humanistic psychologies.
- Transpersonal psychologies, including the Jungian approach, point out the need for meaning and purpose in life, and certainly depression can result from the lack of life purpose and meaningfulness, or equally from the feeling of being impeded in the achievement of that purpose.
- Finally, depth psychology points to a depressed person's difficulty in reaching out to others to make meaningful contact. A feeling of isolation and being walled in results. It is easy to see the close connection between this difficulty and the unconscious feeling of despair over not having been able to reach out to one's mother for loving contact early in life.

Aside from understanding the etiological background of depression, it is important to find out how the person *uses* the particular difficulty for certain emotional effects, whether intrapsychic or interpersonal. Therapists call this the *secondary gain* of the condition.

For example, an individual can use depression in any one of several ways: to gain sympathy or support, to get revenge, to prove to himself how harsh or cruel the world is and therefore avoid the risk of asserting himself and reaching out. As one patient told me, "I would acquiesce in what people wanted me to do whether I wanted to or not, resent it, close off to them, and then feel angry and revengeful inside. In the end, I would feel secretly victorious but depressed." All of this was an internal struggle to assuage a long-ago hurt from the parents and satisfy a need for revenge, meanwhile keeping the struggle secret. The psychotherapy patient often knows intuitively that to reveal his innermost feelings in the present he would appear inappropriate, childish, or out of control. Yet often enough, the deepest progress occurs when the patient finally allows himself to be inappropriate and childish.

One key factor in the need to maintain the low ego, and low energy of depression is that getting out of a depressed way of life means genuine change in behavior and self-image, the loss of old structures and defenses, and the development of unpleasant feelings of insecurity and anxiety. Depression, if it is not intense, is always more tolerable than anxiety.

Some psychotherapists focus in on the secondary-gain aspect of the symptom as a key therapeutic maneuver. They will confront the patient with a strong question: "What do you get out of it? What is the advantage for you?" This sometimes challenges the patient to face more courageously defensive and routine attitudes involved in the depressive structure. On the other hand, if the therapist utilizes confrontation of the possible secondary gains in an overly standardized way, not doing justice to the depths and difficulty of the block, she can easily make the patient even more self-critical. Even though there are general patterns and dynamics that are applicable to everyone, a standard, uniform approach can never work, since psychological difficulties are not only multidimensional but individual.

Astrologers, as well as psychotherapists, will often point out to clients the need to get in touch with their Mars energy, their anger and assertiveness, as one way to alleviate depression. But again there arises the question of readiness. If the person's self-image is poor and his ability to make contact with others for emotional exchange is diminished, then the expression of anger will tend to increase the depression, since this kind of person cannot tolerate the increased energy charge of the expression of anger nor the threat to relationships and self-image.

It is important for the astrologer to assess the severity of the depression. A chronically limiting depressive quality in a client or a severe acute depression should always be referred to a competent psychotherapist. A mildly depressed, or even moderately depressed client could be helped, however, by occasional visits to an astrological counselor for security, clarification, and support. It is important that the particular astrologer have good counseling tools and have a good heart. Here, especially, each situation is unique, and it is difficult to establish general guidelines. Clients who feel that astrology is philosophically more meaningful to them than psychotherapy, who fear the "dredging-up" aspect of therapy and feel a real emotional contact with an astrologer could probably be helped more in the astrological situation than in the psychotherapeutic one. The drawback of this kind of situation, however, is that the astrological client who is really depressed yet resistant to psychotherapy will tend to become more and more dependent on the astrologer and will put pressure on the astrologer for frequent visits and therefore the establishment of a psychotherapeutic relationship.

It is not a simple thing to offer general suggestions about behavioral changes or life activities that people can undertake in order to come out of a depressive phase. One person might feel better from taking a new job with more responsibility if it satisfies her need for accomplishment and recognition, whereas another might be better off leaving a job of responsibility and pressure if that job was in fact too great a task for the person to handle effectively and presented a continual threat of failure and diminished self-image. One person can begin to feel better about himself by learning to express anger, since that means standing up for himself and releasing pent-up feelings, whereas another person might feel better by giving up a tendency to rash anger if the anger has always led to unresolved arguments and was a defense against fear or hurt and being able to recognize deeper needs and attitudes.

But there are specific psychotherapeutic tools that are

especially helpful in the relief of depression (or any other psychological disturbance, for that matter). A consistently supportive, nonjudgmental, caring, and understanding attitude on the part of the therapist will provide the necessary emotional security for the development of a belief in the self. From that valuable foundation, therapist and patient can begin to unravel the deep conflicts and fears that constitute the roots of depression.

Emotional release is also vitally necessary, but only if it is brought about when the person is ready and is allowed quieter emotional periods in between for integrating the new material. Readiness is the all-important concept here. It comes through a gradual dissolution of the defenses used by the individual to protect himself against the particular threatening emotions and attitudes. It also implies that there has developed some outlet in the person's life for the newly released emotion, need, and energy charge. Coincident with these signs of the person's growth should be a recognition of the hidden conflicts and needs that lie buried at the source of the emerging feelings, as well as a new, and genuine, assumption of responsibility for his participation in his own life difficulties.

The development of genuine insight and understanding can literally boost a person out of a depressive condition, for it provides her with a feeling that there is a way out of her emotional paralysis and functions as the source of a new sense of identity, meaning, and purpose. The kind of insight I am referring to is not the result of a concerted intellectual effort to understand causes, however. It derives from a balanced emotional and mental experiencing that is the sum of a whole set of new behaviors—venturing new actions, reaching out to others, plus reaching inward more deeply into the self in a probing, honest way.

Psychoanalysis has been rightly accused of actually engendering new problems with its overemphasis on the mental function to the detriment of the emotional, intuitive, and experiential functions. But the insight of which I speak involves a polarity, for one must simultaneously look at one's problems with a keener mental effort and let the opposite happen as well, that is, let go of one's good sense and rationality, take chances, and become completely immersed and "lost" in one's life with openness and emotionality.

Only one generalization seems valid: Depression is the result of blocked energy and emotional movement, both within the person and from the person toward the world. Or, to put it another way, it is a manifestation of the stasis of energy flow and emotional expression that occurs within the context of meaningless activity and self-hatred. Therefore, any purposeful activity that a person believes in can be significant in altering depressive trends.

Unfortunately, modifying a current or acute depressive period, as I have just described, is not the same as changing permanently a deep, chronic-depressive character structure. This can be accomplished only through a gradual therapeutic endeavor aimed at loosening the compulsive defense attitudes that dominate the surface of the psyche (termed the persona or character armor), reliving in an integrateable way repressed emotions and needs from childhood, fulfilling the childhood needs now as an adult that were not met at that time, and thus resolving the childhood conflict hidden under the defenses. For example, a man in therapy might have as his primary conflict a feeling of lack of recognition, approval, and love from his distant, critical father. In the process of reliving, when he is ready, his fear, pain, rage, and longing with the help of an accepting and emotionally contactful therapist, the person will begin to reach out to others for recognition and love in a direct and appropriate way. Part of his childhood need, once it becomes more recognized and expressed, will diminish and eventually disappear, while another part will remain as a component of his mature ego. With the resolution of the childhood conflicts and fulfillment of unmet needs, the person will become integrated. He will gain a genuine sense of self and the capacity for love and creative work, and thus the depressive tendency will no longer have reason to exist.

A case in my therapy practice illustrates the connection

between astrological concepts and those of modern depth psychology. A man in his early thirties came for therapy with problems of chronic depression, social withdrawal, disorganization and impracticality regarding the material demands of life, sexual frustration, and feeling blocked in his work life. He was a college professor with aspirations to be a creative writer and felt limited in both teaching and writing. He had intense, short-lived, and sporadic love affairs and had been married briefly in his early twenties. He had a few close friends but tended to neglect friendships as he found it very difficult to confront people about interpersonal difficulties.

His behavior in the early part of therapy was friendly, talkative, exaggeratedly witty, and very needy. Markedly intelligent and sensitive, he had a soft, yielding manner and appeared to need to win my approval and support at all costs. There was an attempt to reason out his life problems, joke about them, feel confused, and avoid direct emotionality. When he felt depressed, his speech slowed down and his eye expression became cloudy, which expressed a block in being able to take action in life in an effective way about some major issue. Physically, he was thin, with soft musculature and quick movements. The family history revealed that he had felt alienated in his home life. His father was weak, critical, and bland, while his mother was closer to him but controlling.

The keynote qualities of his characterological defenses were: passivity, a need to please, exaggerated humor, intellectual distancing. His emotions and needs, therefore, were stifled with a consequent tendency to depression, contactlessness, and confusion.

Let us examine the natal astrological picture that corresponds to his adult patterns. A strong, sensitive emotional nature can be seen with his Sun in Pisces in the first house trine Jupiter in Cancer in the fifth house. But expression of this strong emotional nature was blocked by the following natal conditions: Saturn is in the fourth house, squaring his Sun, indicating a deep sense of pain and frustration in the home life, conflict with the father, and resulting self-doubt and sense of inadequacy. Mars is in the twelfth house revealing a difficulty in asserting his needs and feelings; and a Moon in Capricorn adds a sense of cautiousness and overstructuring regarding the expression of feeling. Finally, an Aquarius Ascendant with Mercury in Aquarius in the first house added a tendency for the client to hide his true feelings behind intellect and detachment.

Therapeutically, the early part of the therapy moved naturally into an easy sharing of his ideas and experiences, conflicts and wit, confusion and struggle. One of the aims of this early period of the therapy was to attain a sense of reality, contact, support, and beginning real trust with me to overcome the difficult and blocking image of his father. This made it possible for the client to feel more secure in the expression of threatening repressed emotions and thoughts. The next phase of therapy grew organically from the first and consisted of the release of painful emotions and crying, with some frustration and anger. This period corresponded not only to increasing trust and closeness between us but also to the client beginning to let go of the defensive aspects of his humor and intellect. He relied less on my judgment and began to assert himself in new ways. Both work and relationship functions improved. Gradually, the release of bottled-up pain led to a greater expression of anger and rage. The appropriate release of both the vulnerable and aggressive emotions brought a steady improvement of a sense of self, ability to focus and take action, and decreasing depressions.

(The work with this patient on depth emotions and character structure also included a good deal of work on genuine insight, self-concept, dreams, body expression and blocks, transferential phenomena, and so on.)

I have used this case to illustrate some of the basic dynamics of depression: insufficiency of warmth and nurturing in the early years of life, lack of modeling for a good ego, and blockage of the ability to assert oneself. It also shows the correspondence of psychotherapeutic and astrological concepts and aims. It further illustrates how the negative qualities of a sign position or aspect can be transformed into their opposite, positive qualities through life experience, counseling, or psychotherapy.

The interpretive skills of a good astrologer can be helpful to the depressed person and to her psychotherapist alike. The deeply symbolic meanings contained in the natal configurations reveal the nature of the hidden conflicts that form the background of the depression. With them the person can be helped to reach greater insight. Knowing the natal capacities, the astrologer can also help with informed suggestions of various ways to stimulate and activate the individual in the present. And finally, astrologers have a wonderful tool in their ability to point out the significance and duration of transits, for the knowledge that a current difficult period will not last can afford a troubled person much relief and security.

11

The Client with
Serious Psychopathology

The astrologer is called upon to work with a large variety of clients. These range from stable, competent persons who want an educational overview of their psychological patterns to insecure, frightened individuals who need a considerable degree of help on many levels. Some of the latter will not reveal the seriousness of their emotional condition until a professional relationship is already established with the astrologer. The astrologer then needs to know how to handle difficult situations of this kind, how to assess the extent of his or her own competency in counseling, and when to refer a client to a psychotherapist.

There are two basic ways the astrologer can assess serious emotional difficulty in a client in addition to the insights provided by the astrological information: client behavior during the consultation and the reported history and life patterns of the client.

Behavior of the Client During the Consultation

By serious psychopathology I am not indicating a psychosis or predisposition to psychosis, although this could be one eventuality. I am referring to serious emotional conflicts and blocks that are beyond the counseling scope of the astrologer and require psychotherapeutic efforts. Everyone has some background of emotional conflict, and the tensions and struggles to overcome and understand them can increase awareness and psychological depth. The conflicts become psychopathological when they become so pervasive and pressuring as to disturb the ability for growth, satisfaction, and awareness of the individual and the ability to cope with the realities of living.

A client can hide a fairly serious neurosis during an initial consultation by maintaining a convincing social role or polite behavior. At times, however, signs of an underlying serious conflict can emerge. The following behaviors give some indications.

Severe Body Tension

The connection between chronic body tension and repressed emotional conflict is well known to most people. What is not so clear are the many complexities and subtleties involved.

For the astrological counselor it would be a valid estimate that a client with moderate to severe body tension will require psychotherapy. A person who is evidently suffering from an inner awareness of tension and emotional conflict probably is not coping as well with life demands as a person who is not aware of his tense state; however, the former individual, whose defenses are less successful, is often a better candidate for genuine change in therapy.

Though it can generally be said that the degree of chronic tension is equal to the depth of insecurity, there are important exceptions. Certain types of individuals can have relatively little chronic tension but still have a serious emotional block. (Using traditional analytic terminology, they are: the oral-dependent personalities, some hysterics, and some schizophrenic individuals.) These individuals do not have enough generalized body tension to "bind" their energy and emotion, so that a need to discharge their energies and feelings immediately is very strong. But since they are not well-integrated persons, their emotional energy comes out in a scattered, unfocused, or inappropriate way.

Body tension not only represses energy, feeling, and impulse, but also reflects psychological attitudes. For example, an individual who is very arrogant will carry himself with an erect, tight back, a tight neck, and a haughty expression around the eyes and mouth; a depressed, submissive person will very likely have a deflated chest, diminished expression in the eyes, voice, and face, and limited respiration. To some extent these correlations are common sense, but most people don't credit their own intuition about this. Knowledge of body language is gradually becoming a more systematic part of contemporary psychotherapy. The psychiatrist most responsible for its development was Wilhelm Reich.

Limited Eye Contact

A difficulty in the client in establishing and maintaining a comfortable eye contact with the astrological counselor can indicate a deep personality block. The eyes are truly "mirrors of the soul." Some ways in which this difficulty manifests are: a rigid, fixed eye expression; eyes that tend to stare through a person; darting, unsteady eyes; a dead, unfeeling expression; a frightened, childlike expression.

The eyes express the emotional state, whether it be alive and contactful or blocked and disturbed. Similar statements can be made about the vocal expression, for it, like the eyes, is a significant indicator of internal life.

Distractible Behavior and Strong Emotional Responses

This question of recognizing and dealing with seriously disturbed behavior again illustrates my contention that the astrological counselor can benefit from counseling training, psychology courses, and personal therapy experience. Take, for example, the situation in which a client cries during a consultation when discussing an area of his or her life. Even a fairly well-grounded person who is experiencing a current stressful problem, does not have an outlet for her emotions, and feels particularly understood and accepted by the astrologer might act this way occasionally. But it also could happen to be a very fragile, lonely individual who feels the astrologer is a caring parent substitute. Many variations of meaning can be present in the strong expression of emotion, and the astrologer should know how to handle it, at the same time exploring the current inner life, outer circumstances, and general life patterns of the individual in order to best assess the degree of severity of emotional dysfunction.

Similarly, a client who becomes angry during an astrological consultation can be expressing one of several possible meanings: He may be paranoid and see the astrologer as a threatening figure; he may be expressing rebellious feelings toward authority figures, he may be experiencing the beginning of a breakdown of psychological defenses; he may be frustrated with the astrologer due to a disharmony between their personalities or unwarranted expectations of his own; or quite simply, he may be expressing frustration about a life circumstance because he feels particularly understood and accepted by the astrologer. Again, the astrologer has to be able to respond to hostility or anger in an effective way and also have some idea of the possible meanings of such behavior.

Suggestive Verbal Content

Here we are dealing with the content and style of speech of the client. Suggestions of marked inner psychological difficulty can vary from hesitant, illogical, or wandering statements to responses that are evasive or camouflaging of real issues. Specific statements can be indicative: "Sometimes I feel the world is falling apart" reveals a projection of an inner perception of psychological collapse or the potential for it. "I often don't know who I am" is said by a person who feels depersonalized or detached from his or her inner state.

It is rare or unlikely that the astrologer will encounter a client in an overt psychotic state with delusions and hallucinations, who is experiencing a break from external reality and has no barriers to the unconscious world. It is more likely that the astrologer will see an occasional "borderline" personality (a person who can be placed diagnostically between "neurosis" and "psychosis"). This kind of person usually makes sense when he talks and is in touch with the world around him, but tends to swing between unwarranted remarks of self-exaltation and self-depreciation and have limited personal and work functions. More typically, the astrologer needs to be aware of remarks from clients that show feelings of not being able to cope, of poor sense of self-worth, and of exaggerated fears of the world. The astrologer has to be able to assess the real meaning and depth of these kinds of remarks within the limits of her role.

History of the Client's Behavior Outside the Consultation

My understanding from astrologers is that overtly difficult client behavior like I have just described is fairly atypical. The current and past life history and attitudes of the clients as well as the invaluable information obtained from the natal chart, progressions, and transits constitute the more likely source of information about the client's present psychological status.

Recent History of Anxiety and/or Depression

A history of periods of intense anxiety and/or depression is indicative of emotional disturbances as well as of the presence of important psychological content. In general, in depression there is the tendency to give up the struggle of living and the existence of self-hatred, whereas in anxiety there is more push for activity and life but with internal conflict and fear. When depression lifts, the potential for excitement occurs, but with that comes the development of anxiety.

Intense and long-lasting periods of depression and/or anxiety are indicative of severe emotional and psychological problems. A certain degree of occasional anxiety is considered healthy if it corresponds to the reasonable demands or threats of the situation. For instance, it is natural to feel somewhat anxious when applying for a job or taking a test. Unhealthy anxiety is of greater intensity and duration than the objective situation warrants and is due to unconscious symbolic fears. Many psychologists consider the question of anxiety to be the most crucial one in the mental health field.

Some individuals are exceedingly vulnerable to new stress and anxiety when they have had little experience with anxiety, while another individual will handle a disappointment or frustration with greater ease, as he has adapted to some degree of conflict and anxiety.

Work History

A history of difficulty in establishing a meaningful direction in one's work sometimes indicates a severe inner block. The exceptions to this are those highly talented, original individuals who often find it difficult to discover their particular path until later in life.

Let us compare two individuals of the same age and with similar difficulties in establishing a work life. Their different attitudes can help illustrate some important elements of people's differing potentials.

One man, aged thirty, has worked at several jobs but has not established a convincing direction for himself. He has several genuine interests, makes lasting friendships, and aspires to genuine self-knowledge and growth. In consultation with the astrologer, he shows eagerness to learn as much about himself as possible, including the more difficult areas. He makes good eye contact. In discussing his work history, he explains the many vicissitudes as ways he has gained more life experience and self-knowledge. Of such a hypothetical individual we can expect a possible resolution of his career difficulties.

Another person reports a similar inability to establish a career direction. This man, however, feels that the job difficulties are usually due to difficult bosses and co-workers and boring tasks. The emphasis is on other people as a cause of the problem. Furthermore, he has had a hard time maintaining friendships. Extensive periods of anxiety and depression are reported. During the consultation eye contact is hesitant, and the discussion of most topics does not proceed to a reasonable conclusion. In this person, deep, structural problems run deeper than they did in the individual first described, and there is less likelihood of the eventual establishment of a satisfying work life.

From this I hope it is clear that the particular problem is not really the issue and can be evaluated only by understanding the whole person.

Relationships

The ability to form and maintain significant relationships is also an important indicator of emotional functioning. This refers to both love relationships involving sexual union and deep friendships. In general, a person who has relationships has a better sense of self and is functioning in a healthier way than a person who does not. However, the astrologer should be aware of the limitations of generalities, for there is the well-known exception of the person who has had a long-term relationship, has hidden herself within it, and with its ending does very poorly emotionally. Then again there is the person who has had a series of relationships, none of them long-lasting, but has worked at personal growth and awareness throughout, has developed a deeper sense of self, and finally achieves a significant relationship. So complex and so various are the issues involved here that the question is really beyond the scope of this book. Suffice it to say that the astrologer should be looking not only for the client's ability to maintain a relationship but also for whether it helps the person to grow on many levels.

12

Problems Created by the Astrologer

The field of astrological counseling deals with human beings in need who are coming to a professional for clarification and guidance. Every aspect of the person can be touched upon in an astrological consultation from the most general to the most specific and intimate. This requires that the astrologer be not only competent in her or his field but relatively mature, objective, sensitive, and compassionate. This is a tall order, hard to maintain at all times, and situations are bound to arise in which unresolved psychological aspects of the astrologer can influence the consultation for the worse.

In the field of psychotherapy, this kind of interaction has been written about extensively and includes what is called *countertransference*.* Since neither therapists nor astrologers are gods, nor are they even fully realized human beings, there is a possibility that unconscious aspects of the therapist will be triggered off and focused by certain types of patients and situations and that, consequently, optimum therapy may not be achieved.

The field of astrology is particularly vulnerable to these difficulties because of astrologers' lack of training in counseling and because of the power the client gives the astrologer by believing that he or she is perfectly able to interpret the astrological information without the client's participation.

Countertransference refers to the situation where a therapist projects into the therapy relationship unresolved needs and feelings of his or her own, particularly those originating toward the parents.

Suggesting One's Own Omniscience

Latent in the astrological consultation is a potent combination of forces, easily misused: On the one hand you have an impressive body of knowledge derived from esoteric sources, and on the other, a searching, needy person with a desire to seek a magical and immediate solution. The astrologer with a weak ego or a poor sense of responsibility can easily be stimulated by this to want to claim for herself an excessive sense of power and omniscience. Such a usurpation of power affects both the client and the astrologer, however. If the client is at all fragile and impressionable, he can become too dependent on the astrologer, too affected by everything she says, and can begin to feel that his natal chart and planetary influences are all-determining, that he has no power or free will of his own. The astrologer, in turn, can limit her ability to grow by denying herself one of the greatest sources of self-development: acceptance of one's mistakes and limitations.

In fact, the bad reputation astrology must contend with is partly due to those astrologers who make definite predictions about people's death, divorce, or illness, and other statements that suggest the client must suffer the rest of his life with a difficult psychological problem in order to correct a karmic imbalance. Such astrologers are exhibiting arrogance and insensitivity in the extreme. Stephen Arroyo, in his book *Astrology, Psychology, and the Four Elements*, says,

> The fact that some astrologers continue to play the role of fortune teller or all knowing channel for cosmic wisdom is merely an indication that such astrologers have their ego too wrapped up in that role. Astrologers, no matter how they see themselves or how the public may view them, are merely human beings like any others, with limited knowledge, limited understanding, and limited experience.[7]

---

[7] Stephen Arroyo, *Astrology, Psychology, and the Four Elements* (Reno, Nevada: CRCS Publications, 1975), p. 52. Available from the publisher of this book.

The need to suggest one's own omniscience, and the ego and power problems implied, are common in those who play the role of helper/healer in the field of psychological and spiritual problems. Therapist, astrologer, psychic, spiritual counselor— all are prone to this difficulty (although many have managed to overcome it). Some of the dynamics of this all-too-human tendency are the following.

Sense of Superiority

The psychiatrist Alfred Adler's theory is based on the observation that many people have the need to feel superior as a compensation for deeper feelings of inadequacy and inferiority. Astrologers find that a feeling of respect and authority accrues to them simply by virtue of their role as conveyor of a profound knowledge and that this can give them, particularly beginning astrologers, a sense of easily won importance and power. If there are significant inner feelings of low self-esteem, then the need for maintaining the sense of superiority is all the more urgent. Unconsciously, the fear is that if the superior attitude is surrendered at all, then the opposite feelings of inadequacy will overwhelm the ego.

Maintaining the superior position also keeps the professional from recognizing his or her own unconscious fear of the loss of control and power, with its consequent feeling of powerlessness. The fear of powerlessness, in turn, refers back to the perception one had of oneself as a child. If the helpless and dependent needs of infancy were not met and the natural expressions of strength, independence, and individuality were also denied an outlet, then the person would have such a feeling buried within him and expressed as body tension. The sense of superiority acts to mask that.

There is another theory of the origin of the superior attitude that seems to contradict the explanation I have just advanced but, when looked at more carefully, actually supports it. The theory of childhood omnipotence ("I cry, and mother comes immediately and whenever I want"). The reason for this is that the development of the child's narcissistic sense derives from the fact of an anxious or ambivalent response from the environment to the child's needs. In consequence, the child keeps demanding more attention in her search for genuine satisfaction, but she does not obtain it because of the insufficiency of the internal attitude of the parent. As a result the person develops a large ego without the underlying conviction of its basis in reality. The omniscient and omnipotent attitude of the adult is sometimes the reflection of this kind of childhood situation.

Perfectionism

Another ingredient of the omniscient attitude so frequently found in the professional is the need to be correct at all times. This is a general human tendency, of course, but it is aggravated in astrology, unfortunately, by the demand on the part of clients for absolute answers.

Again we can look to childhood experience for some of the origins of this tendency. When parents demand consistently "correct" behavior from the child, the need to be absolutely correct often develops. The opposite tendency—the need to rebel and be incorrect—can also occur, of course. But if it gets repressed, as is often the case, it becomes a feared impulse to misbehave and thus gives rise to a generalized, underlying guilt, which only reinforces the need to be perfect.

Parents who do not demand so much perfection from the child but are overly demanding of themselves only teach it to the child by example, which is not much better.

The roots of the tendency to perfectionism extend further than childhood experience, however. Certainly the Protestant ethic and the Judeo-Christian tradition have fostered such attitudes. And it has even been suggested that the origin of perfectionism goes back as far as the earliest development of patriarchal society, with its repression of the animal instincts in human beings.

Emotional Distance

An important effect of the stance of being a superior authority, on the interpersonal level, is to put the professional at an emotional distance from the client. This distance safeguards the helper from being influenced by the personality of the client, so that undesirable aspects of the professional herself will not be stimulated. Thus, the pretense of omniscience can act like a protective cocoon.

The necessity for the astrologer or therapist to maintain an objective and professional posture is carried to an exaggerated degree and becomes authoritarian when the helper begins to believe she is all-knowing. The fact that the person has an important knowledge of theory and technique and therefore is a kind of authority does not mean that this person has all the answers, is invulnerable, and cannot make meaningful contact. Genuine personal relating that takes place in a counseling or therapy setting does not necessarily entail the loss of objectivity. What such a fear really means is that the professional doesn't trust his or her personal nature to be shown at all.

Playing the Parent

The desire to be oracular or omniscient as an astrologer is one form of being an all-powerful parent, but only certain types of people fall prey to this. Others satisfy parental strivings, instead, by being overprotective. Many clients come to the consultation with a need for support and direction as well as clarification, and the astrologer becomes a parent when she or he takes this function beyond certain limits. (I have gone into this at greater length in Chapter 9, on dependency problems of the client.)

A parental attitude on the part of the healer/helper is sometimes related to a need to usurp the authority of one's parents, to do a kind of symbolic one-upmanship on them. In that case, the attempt to act the part of a parent is related, as well, to the need to be omniscient, which I discussed in the previous section.

Intruding One's Own Philosophy

A study of astrologers' writings and lectures shows that astrologers sometimes combine strictly astrological concepts with ideas from nonastrological philosophies, psychologies, and other disciplines. Among these are Eastern philosophies; Western esoteric thought; psychological schools such as those of Freud, Jung, Gestalt, psychosynthesis; wholistic health concepts; forms of meditation; and various scientific concepts. All of this is inevitable and often broadens the astrological literature. It can be harmful to the client, however, when a particular philosophy or practice is so strongly advocated by the astrologer that the client feels he is failing in living up to his potential if he doesn't take up the astrologer's suggestions.

A twenty-seven-year-old male patient of mine had a basic horoscope analysis with an astrologer. Although he said he felt that the various descriptions of his psychological patterns were quite accurate, he complained of feeling discouraged. After some probing, I discovered the cause. It seems that, from the chart analysis and the client's description of his present life and problems, the astrologer felt my patient had great potentials that he was not tapping and that this appeared to be due to a strong spiritual bent he was ignoring. She urged him to begin meditating. He thought that perhaps she was right, but in the days that followed realized that he had little inclination to meditate or even to learn the practice. As a result he began to feel that he was not willing to help himself or must be cowardly or terribly lazy. (He happened to have been a very impressionable Cancerian.) If it had not been for our discussion of the event and its implications, he might have retained a degree of discouragement for some time.

I am convinced that this astrologer could have achieved more constructive results if she had described the man's potential to him and then simply asked him for his reactions to her observations. This would have created a more open dialogue, in which she could even have suggested meditation along with other alternatives as possible avenues of self-growth, but with the understanding that he might find other means for his development, too. As a sensitive, self-critical, and aspiring young person, he would then not be likely to take what she said as the only way of growth open for him.

Putting Forth a Bland Positivism

Another basic problem is the tendency of a certain type of astrologer to focus on only the "positive" aspects of the client's chart. Such an astrologer treats the conflictual parts of the natal chart as "wonderful opportunity for growth" (which it is) and neglects the disturbing possibilities of the client's personality.

It is true that a certain minority of clients have so poor a self-image that a positive, supportive, underplaying of the difficult parts of the chart is called for. This is a sensitive and therapeutic approach. Where a therapeutic positivism begins to be an avoidance of the "dark side of the soul," and thereby a kind of overspiritualizing, is when the astrologer attempts to deny or diminish all of the client's tendencies to negativism, that is, any critical or angry attitudes or feelings toward others, the self, or life in general.

It seems to me that the subject of "the negative" is a crucial one, and also highly complex. Certainly, to approach all negative reactions of the client as something to be corrected is a sure road to superficiality, or, if nothing more, a failure to move toward wholeness and reality, on the part of both client and astrologer. In truth, much of our anger, rage, and hatred resolve down to a healthy power and love that have been blocked. Sidestepping the negative feelings does not allow for the regeneration of those positive feelings that lie at the core. It is only through genuine acceptance of these difficult feelings, at a time when a person has a sufficiently strong sense of self-worth, that the necessary reliving of the original conflicts and frustrations can occur to help overcome the block.

There are appropriate situations when the correction of a "negative" attitude might be warranted. They are the following: (a) when the client continually focuses on the unpleasant aspects of the other person in a relationship in order to avoid recognizing his or her own problematic behavior; (b) when a client habitually downgrades his life and behavior; and (c) when a client habitually criticizes a segment of society to avoid dealing with that kind of person or that quality in himself. Yet, even though such negative attitudes need to be changed, the way to accomplish that is not easy and clear. For example, if a client complains to the astrologer that she is a failure or a poor prospect as a lover, to tell the client that her negative attitude only reinforces her difficulty will likely have little success. Chances are that she has already been told this by friends and has read the idea in books or articles. If anything were to help in a short-term counseling situation, it would be to ask the client to speak more at length about how she is a failure, listening with objectivity and empathy. This would help her begin to see *for herself* the psychodynamics behind, and perhaps the meaning of, her negative attitude.

Failing to Recognize
One's Own Unresolved Conflicts

Since everyone has some kind of persistent internal conflict, if only minimally, it is understandable that certain types of clients will activate those areas of the astrologer's internal life. This does not have to interfere with the counseling as long as the astrologer is aware of his own unresolved conflict and has the objectivity and rational control to temper his reactions and attitudes. Some of the more typical sensitive areas of clients that can challenge or threaten astrologers are: easily expressed anger and hatred toward others; feelings of inadequacy and failure in professional, interpersonal, or sexual functions; fears of vulnerability and pain; extreme childlike needs; emotional overcontrol of oneself; tendencies to domination and submission; sexual-role issues and tendencies to sexual promiscuity; marital and divorce issues; parent-child relations.

As the astrologers in the ongoing sharing group that I have

described earlier have noted, there tends to be a remarkable synchronicity (or simultaneity of occurrence) between a pattern in the particular type of client who calls or type of presenting client problem and the kind of issues the astrologer is currently dealing with in himself. It can therefore afford an excellent opportunity for self-learning and growth for the astrologer.

Astrologers can become aware that a sensitive personal area is being touched off. The presence in them of any of the following reactions should give them a significant clue:

- Becoming angry and impatient with the client
- Feeling intense pain for a difficult plight of a client
- Avoiding crucial areas of the client's chart
- Frequently giving one-directional advice
- Yielding to many demands for extra time
- Giving long speeches to the client or having arguments

There are exceptions to any rule, of course, and there will be occasions when an astrologer's behavior mirrors one of the preceding conditions yet does not represent a chronic conflict within him or her. Let these points merely serve as guideposts—or warning lights—to the unresolved depths that join astrologer and client in a common humanity.

Conclusion: Astrology and Psychotherapy Revisited

The connections between astrology and psychotherapy that I have tried to sketch through this book are in fact much more intricate and deserve a broader canvas, a richer palette. And there are many angles of perspective from which to summarize them.

From one point of view we can see how the methods the astrologer and the psychotherapist use to help the searching individual *contrast* with one another. The astrologer helps essentially by clarifying for the client his basic patterns and their significance as shown by the natal chart and focused by current cyclic influences. Thus, by recognizing the true nature of his psychological potential, as well as the significance of present-day opportunities and stresses, the individual gains the security and self-awareness that help him see struggles as meaningful sources of growth.

The psychotherapist, by contrast, has no immediately available tool of clarification. She does, however, have useful concepts for the interpretation of intrapsychic conflict and development. She also has valuable therapeutic techniques that can open the doors of the psyche to the repressed conflicts and emotions. Unfortunately, these tools of interpretation and technique cannot be used at the beginning of the therapeutic process, because the unique *gestalt* of the individual must be thoroughly understood first, a more gradual process.

I strongly feel that the therapist should provide a consistently objective and supportive atmosphere for the unburdening of stressful and repressed thoughts, emotions, impulses, images, memories, and fantasies. The release of these difficult internal states, if done correctly, leads to depth insight and a strengthening of the sense of self. In the process, the searching

individual can begin to take ownership of the various conflicting parts, archetypes, and subpersonalities of the total self in
order gradually to transform and harmonize them.

In sum, whereas astrology helps with immediate clarification, therapy helps with emotional release, relationship, and the
gradual development of insight.

Another way of looking at astrology and psychotherapy is
to consider the *similarities* between the two fields. If we were
to delete from an astrological consultation the use of specific
astrological terms, then we would hear language and concepts
that a good therapist could employ. The needs, energies, and
principles expressed by the planets, Sun, and Moon are the
same as those investigated in depth psychotherapy. Both the
astrologer and the therapist concern themselves with assertion,
anger, and sexuality (Mars); the need to control, let go, and
transform (Pluto); the "contraction" of pain, frustration, and
withdrawal (Saturn); love, gratification, and relationship needs
(Venus); emotional responsiveness (Moon); ways of perceiving,
thinking, and communicating (Mercury); and so on. The concerns are often the same, though the astrologer will frequently
have an additional metaphysical and spiritual outlook that
many therapists do not have.

Furthermore, both the astrologer and the therapist are
aware of the ways in which these diverse energies and qualities
are sometimes in conflict and out of balance. And both know
that growth and selfhood are achieved by working toward
balance and inner harmony, that is, by resolving conflicts in a
conscious, responsible way, not by avoiding or dulling them.
The astrologer might tell the client that the combined effects
of the transiting planets are acting to force him to face himself
and his habitual patterns and recognize his opportunities for
growth. The therapist might say that the pain, frustration, and
lack of gratification in the person's life force him to confront
worn-out structures, defenses, and hidden elements of his
personality. Astrologer and therapist alike are concerned with
achieving balance between the assertive and the receptive

modes, the inner and the outer persons, the objective and the emotional selves, the functions of intellect, feeling, intuition, and sensation.

A third way to look at the connections between astrology and psychotherapy is to notice the growing possibility of their *mutual enrichment*. In Parts 2 and 3 of this book I outlined the ways in which astrological counseling can benefit from the concepts and techniques of the modern psychologies, psychotherapy, and nonastrological counseling. What was not discussed in any detail, since it is beyond the scope of this book, is the significant contribution astrology can make to psychotherapy. What I would like to see, and I believe it is already beginning to happen, is the recognition among psychotherapists of the validity of astrology so that the two disciplines can work hand in hand for the deeper understanding of people in general and for the more effective aid of disturbed individuals in particular.

Let me conclude by presenting a final perspective, a structural and dynamic view of the psyche that is held implicitly by various schools of psychotherapy (and explicitly by the Jungian and Reichian schools) and that can help to illumine the psychological meanings contained within an astrological chart.

The tridimensional picture of the psyche is roughly similar to the glyph for the Sun in astrology (the circle with a central point). It also corresponds to the diagram of the cell: membrane, protoplasm, and nucleus. The outer circle represents the outer part of the personality that one presents to the world. It is that which helps one function and cope with both the outer and the inner worlds. The middle part of the psyche, beneath the surface personality, is the threatening, "reprehensible" part of the personality that the individual has learned to control and repress. And deeper still, the core or nucleus of the organism, is a healthy, unifying sense of being and individuality that is in touch with nature and the cosmos. The core or center is the true self, at once unique from and similar to all other living creatures.

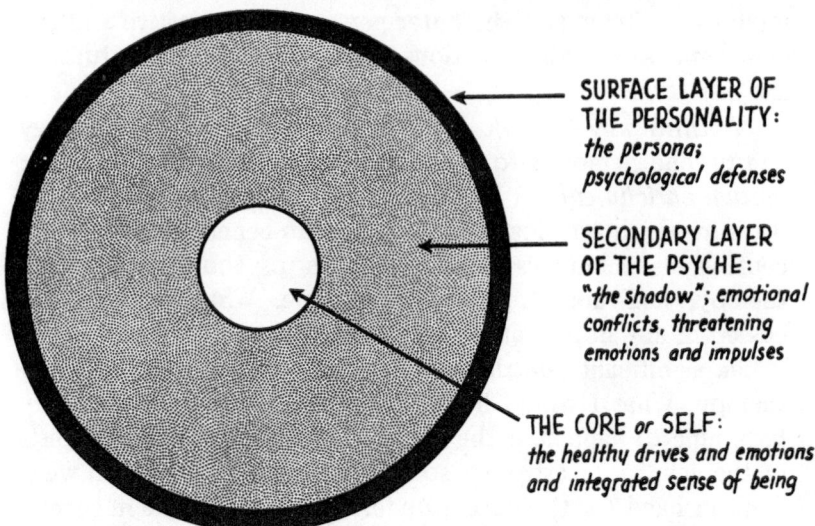

SURFACE LAYER OF
THE PERSONALITY:
the persona;
psychological defenses

SECONDARY LAYER
OF THE PSYCHE:
"the shadow"; emotional
conflicts, threatening
emotions and impulses

THE CORE *or* SELF:
the healthy drives and emotions
and integrated sense of being

This diagram is an adaptation of Wilhelm Reich's description of the human condition.

The surface layer of the psyche has been variously called *the persona, mask, social role, character armor,* and *psychological defenses.* This surface layer is expressive and integrative as well as protective. In its protective or defensive function, it shields one from threatening impulses, emotions, and ideas coming from deeper parts of the personality, at the same time that it does not allow the outer world to see the unpleasant parts of oneself. It also protects the integrity of the personality from overly stressful stimuli from the world, since these pressures could challenge the psyche equilibrium and release the threatening repressed material from within.

Defenses and armor can also function at a deeper layer of the psyche, not just in the outer personality. For example, an aggressive, overly confident manner (persona) in a salesman can be a defense against deeper feelings of fear, inadequacy, and passivity. These latter feelings and attitudes, a threat to the equilibrium of the ego structure, if brought out in a supportive therapeutic situation could then be shown to be a defense against an even deeper layer of anger and rage over feelings of impotence. This layer of rage might actually be functioning as a defense against a still-deeper layer of pain and vulnerability due to the loss of love early in childhood.

It is important to note that the persona, or outer layer, varies in quality and degree in different individuals. In the person who is fairly mature and integrated, the persona will have very little defensive function, and the person's outer behavior can express aspects of his deeper self. Another person, with limited emotional resources and a "shaky ego," will present a persona that is far different from the inner reality. Furthermore, one individual, moderately or even maximally defended, will be aware of the difference between his inner self and outer role and will suffer because of this awareness, while another individual will completely identify with his persona because of a dread of facing inner realities. The latter individual, although he avoids pain, will grow less.

Finally, defenses function not only as a protective mechanism but also as expressive outlets; they integrate the psychobiological energy equilibrium. Thus, it is important for therapist and astrologer alike to respect defenses and not to challenge them before the person has a fairly solid replacement for the old pattern. For example, a person with defensive haughtiness, if confronted too early in therapy, would feel criticized, judged, yet be unable to change it and would therefore either reinforce the behavior, becoming sullen and angry, or even withdraw from therapy.

The second, or middle layer, of the psyche, represents the threatening unconscious part of the personality. It is called *the secondary layer* in Reichian theory and *the shadow* in Jungian theory. In the picture of the psyche represented by the Sun glyph, this middle layer corresponds to the part between the outer circle and the center. But it is hardly an empty psychic space, for it is filled with emotions, memories, attitudes, needs, images, complexes, and conflicts. One could think of it as an archeological stratification of buried material, the very existence of which is threatening to consciousness. Part of this middle layer is made up of aggressive, sexual, and dependent tendencies that society and parents find difficult to tolerate, as well as all the associated images and emotions involved. (The "negative" emotions of intense pain and sadness, terror, rage, and hatred are particularly relevant here.)

The third aspect of the tridimensional psyche is the *core, center,* or *self.* It is the deepest, healthiest, and most unifying part of a person's being. The frustration, early in life, of the loving, out-reaching expressions of the core or self produces, by a negative transformation, the secondary layer, which in its turn has to be controlled and transformed into the surface layer of the personality.

Edward C. Whitmont, a Jungian analyst, in his book *The Symbolic Quest,* writes,

> He [Jung] sets up the hypothetical postulate of the Self as the Center as well as the content of the total personality; it is the root upon which the experience and consciousness of individual being arises as a secondary phenomenon. The Self is experienced or related to as a postulated encompassing personality characterized by individual wholeness and expressing a central guidance system directed toward consciousness and therefore is not identical with the center of consciousness. This archetype expresses itself in the form of predestined wholeness, not merely of general human wholeness, but of the specific wholeness of an individual life, which seeks fulfillment.[8]

Wilhelm Reich speaks of a naturalness (the healthy core) in people that has been distorted by artificial, unnatural, cultural, and family influences. This distortion results in the life-negating effect of the character and muscular armors, which impede the free flow of energy, primary emotions, healthy sexuality, and love.

Before discussing the relevance to astrology of the tridimensional view of the personality, I must elucidate, briefly, the concept of ego, an important part of both astrological and psychological language. Astrologers use the concept of ego to

---

[8] Edward C. Whitmont, *The Symbolic Quest* (Princeton, N.J.: Princeton University Press, 1969), pp. 218–19.

refer to the conscious sense of "I," or self-identity, with its vital functions of perception, discrimination, evaluation, control, choice, and integration. Freudian psychoanalytic use of the concept of the ego is similar, but also includes aspects of the unconscious. In psychoanalysis the ego plays the role of mediator between the conflicting demands of the id (instinctual drives and energies), the superego (one's moral sense and ideal aspirations), and external reality. The ego is less profound, whole, and unifying than the self, or core, but is nevertheless a vital aspect of the functioning of the psyche. The following case study will illustrate, I hope, how the concept of the tridimensional psyche can be useful to astrological understanding as well as to psychotherapeutic practice.

A twenty-six-year-old woman, whom we shall call Barbara, came to therapy because of generalized feelings of inadequacy and lack of assertiveness in both career and love relationships. She was talented in several artistic directions but felt blocked and confused about pursuing any one of them. Attractive and vivacious, she was able to become involved in love relationships, but would tend to subvert her needs and feelings to the dominance of the man, then feel hurt and resentful, and conflict would ensue.

Her immediate manner was charming, winsome, softspoken, and accommodating. In the early therapeutic sessions, her reaction to frustration and conflict in her life was partial crying that called for reassurance and comforting, but initially left her feeling weakened. Socially, her behavior could vary from charming and outgoing to shy, self-sacrificing, hesitant, and self-doubtful. The principal block appeared to be a fear of her own power and assertiveness.

The early home life revealed a history of marked quarreling and conflict between the parents, with minimal love and closeness to Barbara. She reacted by both withdrawing into herself and becoming accommodating, in an attempt to be the moderating force to her quarreling parents.

It was apparent that Barbara accentuated her receptive, Yin qualities in order to repress her more aggressive, Yang qualities. This, again, was in response to her painful home life, in which there was so much jarring aggression, unreasonableness, and hurt. As her therapist, I chose to support and foster the repressed aggressiveness as well as the deeper elements of fear and pain. When the underlying emotions and needs began to be revealed, other attitudes, subpersonalities, and archetypal functions came out as well. Barbara was able to unveil these deeper areas of forbidden elements (the shadow, or secondary layer) only gradually as her self-image improved, her work and social relations became strengthened, and rapport and trust developed between us.

To summarize, the persona, or outer layer, of Barbara's psyche was charm, sweetness, submissiveness, and a hyper-reasonableness, whereas the essence of her shadow appeared to be the polar opposite of this: a forceful, aggressive quality on the one hand and a helpless, frightened, needy quality on the other.

In Barbara's natal chart, there is a stellium in Leo, with the Sun at 3° Leo in the twelfth house, the Ascendant at 12° Leo, Venus exactly conjunct the Ascendant, and Pluto at 20° Leo in the first house conjunct to Mercury at 26° Leo. This heavy Leo emphasis at the Ascendant and in the first house, with Venus on the Ascendant, would predispose Barbara to project herself to the world as charming, warm, and sweet. However, the egotistical quality of Leo would have to be repressed because of her underlying fear of assertion, her inferiority feelings, and her self-doubt.

The fear of assertion is shown in Barbara's chart, I believe, by the fact that Mars is in Scorpio in the fourth house exactly square Venus, the Ascendant, and Pluto. In addition, this is part of a T-Square involving Jupiter in Taurus in the tenth house, opposing the Mars in the fourth house, and squaring the Leo first-house planets. Jupiter in the tenth house opposing Mars in the fourth house undoubtedly represents the parents' conflict, among other things, and these conflicts are challenging Barbara's ability to project herself to the world. Barbara's underlying inferiority feelings also affect her ability to assert herself and could be based to a certain degree on her twelfth-house Sun, her Moon in Virgo, and her Uranus in the twelfth house.

The study of Barbara's natal chart in the context of the therapeutic situation, as well as those of other patients, leads me to venture some tentative statements regarding the three-layered picture of the psyche and its astrological correspondences. Several natal configurations can be used by the ego as a defensive function: particularly the Ascendant, any "soft" aspects; dominance of a sign, element, hemisphere, or quadrant; and the sign the Moon is in. Even the "hard," or challenging, aspects can have a defensive function, but they more typically make up the shadow due to their conflictual nature. From this we can set a better understanding of how the T-Square might operate, for its complexity suggests a double function of repression and defense. The focal planet of the T-Square can function in a personality as a dominant mode of expression, but can also "dominate" and control the other two planetary energies as well as the sign qualities opposite the focal planet. The more dominated planetary energies and needs would then function as part of the more feared or repressed, shadow figure. (Tracy Marks's book *How to Handle Your T-Square* is illuminating in this regard. Available from CRCS Publications.)

The Ascendant, astrologers agree, functions most typically as the outer projection of the personality and therefore stands for the persona. Soft aspects, particularly a close-orbed Grand Trine, because of its ease of expression and nonthreatening quality to the ego, can easily function as a defense as well as a gift of expression. This would not be the case if the planets of the Grand Trine were incompatible, for then they would have a more threatening character.

The shadow part of the personality is generally described by the more inaccessible parts of the chart: twelfth-house planets and signs; missing elements and empty hemispheres; intercepted signs; the sign opposite the focal planet of a T-Square; and so forth. Hard aspects, too, often function this way, as well as occasionally defensively.

The emphasis in a chart of a particular sign or element illustrates the way in which the psyche functions on three levels at once. As we have seen in Barbara's case, her stellium in Leo functioned, first, as a defensive barrier or control against fearsome, repressed energies in that it accentuated her natural charm, sweetness, and affability. But this same Leo quality constitutes part of her threatening shadow self, with the Ascendant, Venus, and Pluto involved in an intense T-Square reflecting serious conflicts in her upbringing. In addition, the egotistic and assertive aspects of the Leo archetype are a threat to a submissive persona. Finally, to complete the tridimensional picture, her Leo qualities represent a deep and healthy part of her total self once the persona and shadow (repressing and repressed) are no longer at war.

What depth psychotherapy does, at its best, is to aid the person in becoming aware of the defensive aspects of his or her outer personality, make contact with the threatening, repressed parts of the deeper self, express and discharge aspects of this threatening force, and gradually allow transformation to a true sense of self.

Finally, it is important to state that the simple psychic schema that I have been referring to necessarily misrepresents the picture in one vital respect. Because it is flat, it reveals no depth. In actually, as we proceed downward, into the depths of the soul, heart, and body of a person, the psyche expands. Although many of the deeper elements are of a destructive nature, once these shadow qualities are expressed in an appropriate, therapeutic way, they become transformed into their underlying positive function (aggression into strength, submissiveness into receptivity). At the core, the person is actually a deeper, broader being, at once animal, human, and divine. A progressive astrology and psychotherapy can work together to aid people in achieving this true sense of self.

Suggested Readings

Freud:

Sigmund Freud
Introductory Lectures on Psychoanalysis
W. W. Norton & Co., 1966

Charles Brenner
An Elementary Textbook of Psychoanalysis
Doubleday & Co., 1957

Norman Cameron
Personality Development and Psychopathology
Houghton Mifflin Co., 1963

Clara Thompson, editor
An Outline of Psychoanalysis
A Modern Library Book, 1955

Jung:

Carl Jung
Memories, Dreams, Reflections
Vintage Books, 1965

Carl Jung
Modern Man in Search of a Soul
Harcourt, Brace, Janovich, 1953

Carl Jung, editor
Man and His Symbols
Doubleday & Co., 1964

Edward C. Whitmont
The Symbolic Quest
Princeton University Press, 1969

Reich:

Wilhelm Reich
The Function of the Orgasm
Simon & Schuster, 1973

Wilhelm Reich
Selected Writings
Noonday Press, 1960

Wilhelm Reich
Character Analysis
Farrar, Straus, and Giroux, 1945

Elsworth Baker
Man in the Trap
Avon Books, 1967

Bioenergetics:

Alexander Lowen
Bioenergetics
Penguin Books, 1975

Alexander Lowen
Depression and the Body
Penguin Books, 1972

Alexander Lowen
Fear of Life
Macmillan Publishing, 1980

Transactional Analysis:

Eric Berne
Transactional Analysis in Psychotherapy
Grove Press, 1961

Eric Berne
Games People Play
Grove Press, 1964

Claude Steiner
Scripts People Live
Bantam Books, 1974

Gestalt Therapy:

Fritz Perls
Gestalt Therapy Verbatim
Bantam Books, 1969

Erving and Miriam Polster
Gestalt Therapy Integrated
Vintage Books, 1973

Psychosynthesis:

Roberto Assagioli
Psychosynthesis
Esalen Book, Penguin Books, 1965

Roberto Assagioli
The Act of Will
Esalen Book, Penguin Books, 1973

There are no books written as yet on counseling that are fully appropriate to the needs of the astrologer. Eugene Kennedy, however, has written an excellent introduction to the field; it provides understanding to any practitioner in the healing arts and is called *On Becoming a Counselor* (Continuum Publishing Corp., 1980).* Any of the books of Rollo May and Joseph Campbell would also be helpful to the fullest education of the astrologer.

---

*Available from CRCS Publications, $9.95 paperback.

Eugene Kennedy has also written *Sexual Counseling* (a $6.95 paperback) and *Crisis Counseling,* also available from the publisher of this book, who tries to stock a number of significant counseling titles that are useful for students or practitioners of astrology. Write for current book list and prices.